Praise for
The Military Spouse's Employment Guide:
Smart Job Choices for Mobile Lifestyles

"Military spouses, like their civilian count   career both to augment the family income as we   vever due to the challenges inherent in the milit   ves they often find it more difficult to achieve   gges- tions offered by Janet Farley in this book can o~~ften~~ ~~also~~   , to better manage the obstacles and develop a satisfying career path." – *Sylvia E.J. Kidd, Director of Family Programs, Association of the US Army*

"We are proud to include Janet Farley on our panel of experts. Her extensive knowledge is invaluable to military spouses exploring their career options as well as though trying to stay up to date on new employment trends and resources." – *Sue Hoppin, Founder and President of the National Military Spouse Network and co-author of "A Family's Guide to the Military"*

"There is no doubt that crafting a career alongside your service member can be a challenge. *The Military Spouse's Employment Guide: Smart Job Choices for Mobile Lifestyles* gives military spouses the tools they need to think outside the box of the traditional workforce while empowering them to create a career of which they can be proud." – *Tara Crooks, Co-founder of www.ArmyWifeNetwork.com and co-author of "1001 Things To Love About Military Life"*

"I use Janet's books all the time with my coaching clients. She gives sound advice in an easy to use way! She is a great example of someone that has found her purpose and is doing work that you can tell she loves. She helps military spouses step up and go for what they want in their careers, so amazing! I highly recommend her work!" – *Krista Wells, The Military Spouse Coach*

"Janet Farley not only knows about careers for military spouses, she has forged her own successful career as a military spouse. She covers this topic inside and out, having both expertise and experience. Her knowledge is evident, as is her affinity for her audience. If you're looking for career advice from someone who has been there, you've found the right book." – *Terri Barnes, Spouse Calls Columnist, "Stars and Stripes Newspaper"*

"Janet's new book is the veritable 'bible' of military spouse employment and is essential for anyone like me who needs more fulfillment than making PB&Js and cleaning toilets can provide!" – *Lisa Smith Molinari, Author of "The Meat and Potatoes of Life" blog*

Books by Janet I. Farley

The Military Spouse's Employment Guide:
Smart Job Choices for Mobile Lifestyles

Quick Military Transition Guide:
Seven Steps to Landing a Civilian Job

The Military Spouse's Complete Guide to Career Success:
Finding Meaningful Employment in Today's Global Marketplace

Military-to-Civilian Career Transition Guide (2nd Edition):
The Essential Job Search Handbook for Service Members

Military-to-Civilian Career Transition Guide:
The Essential Job Search Handbook for Service Members

Jobs and the Military Spouse (2nd Edition):
Married, Mobile and Motivated for the New Job Market

Jobs and the Military Spouse:
Married, Mobile, and Motivated for Employment

The Military Spouse's Employment Guide

Smart Job Choices for Mobile Lifestyles

Janet I. Farley

Impact Publications
Manassas Park, VA

Copyright © 2012 by Janet I. Farley. All rights reserved. Printed in the United States of America. No part of this book may be used or reproduced in any manner whatsoever without written permission of the publisher: IMPACT PUBLICATIONS, 9104 Manassas Drive, Suite N, Manassas Park, VA 20111, Tel. 703-361-7300 or Fax 703-335-9486.

Warning/Liability/Warranty: The author and publisher have made every attempt to provide the reader with accurate, timely, and useful information. However, given the rapid changes taking place in today's economy, some of the author's information will inevitably change. The information presented here is for reference purposes only. The author and publisher make no claims that using this information will guarantee the reader success. The author and publisher shall not be liable for any losses or damages incurred in the process of following the advice in this book.

ISBN: 978-1-57023-333-3 (13-digit); 1-57023-333-0 (10-digit)

Library of Congress: 2011944066

Publisher: For information on Impact Publications, including current and forthcoming publications, authors, press kits, online bookstore, and submission requirements, visit the left navigation bar on the front page of the publisher's main company website: www.impactpublications.com.

Publicity/Rights: For information on publicity, author interviews, and subsidiary rights, contact the Media Relations Department: Tel. 703-361-7300, Fax 703-335-9486, or email: query@impactpublications.com.

Sales/Distribution: All bookstore sales are handled through Impact's trade distributor: National Book Network, 15200 NBN Way, Blue Ridge Summit, PA 17214, Tel. 1-800-462-6420. All special sales and distribution inquiries should be directed to the publisher: Sales Department, IMPACT PUBLICATIONS, 9104 Manassas Drive, Suite N, Manassas Park, VA 20111-5211, Tel. 703-361-7300, Fax 703-335-9486, or email: query@impactpublications.com.

Table of Contents

Dedication

This book is respectfully dedicated to all
military spouses who are working hard in their jobs
or are working hard to get one.

Acknowledgments

Thanks to these people for their assistance and support in writing this book:

Ron Krannich and Mardie Younglof of Impact Publications. For over ten years now, we have worked together as team and made a positive difference with many military spouses and their families. Thank you for giving me that first opportunity to become an author and for allowing me to continue on my personal mission with our successful books. I'd also like to thank Carol S. Cable of CSC Creations for the wonderful work on the graphics and layout of this book.

Marty Emory. You are a great connector of ideas and people and you set the example for the rest of us. Thank you.

Everyone should have a job that she loves. I do. As a freelance writer and careers consultant, I get to write for some fantastic organizations that I am proud to be affiliated with. The Military Officer's Association of America (MoAA), www.moaa.org, is one of them. MoAA is a professional association for military officers and their families at every stage of life and career. They serve everyone in the greater military family, through their tireless legislative efforts and through the MoAA Scholarship Fund. Since 2005, I have authored the Homefront column and periodic features for MoAA. I am eternally grateful to Warren Lacy for giving me that first opportunity and for the editorial expertise through the years of Molly Wyman and most recently, Willow Nero. I am also grateful for the professional support I've received from CDR Rene A. Campos, USN-Retired who currently serves as MoAA's Deputy Director, Government Relations.

I would also like to acknowledge and thank the following people for their support and/or business: Heather Benit and Chad Stewart of the Stars and Stripes Newspapers, Kerry Tucker of Military OneSource, Lindy Kyzer and Eric Pecinovsky of ClearanceJobs.Com, and those who have attended the

Army Community Service (ACS) job search support group that I facilitate in Stuttgart, Germany.

In the course of writing this book, I tapped into the expertise and thoughts of those around me. Thanks to these individuals for theirs: Julie Gifford, Robbie Belesimo, Jeanne Roth, Martha Povich, Kelly Measells, Paula Hallam, Deb Milstein, Kimberly Frady, Linda Benedik, Diana Hartman, Lisa Molinari, and Terri Barnes. My apologizes if I left anyone else off here.

Thanks to Terrie Farley for coming up with the idea of "logitivity" and for letting her mom borrow it for this book.

Finally, I am forever grateful to Farley, Frannie, Terrie, and Bella for reminding me everyday about what matters the most in my life.

The Author

Janet Farley is one of today's leading experts on military spouse and career transition issues and author of six books. She offers servicemembers and their families her own brand of straightforward career management and job search advice based on extensive experience in the outplacement industry and within the Department of Defense. She is a proud U.S. Army military spouse, a U.S. Marine Corps brat, and an advocate for all those who serve in uniform or are married to servicemembers.

Janet writes the "JobTalk" column in the *Stars and Stripes* Newspapers and the "Homefront" column for the Military Officers Association of America (MoAA). Her work has appeared in *CinC-House, Military Spouse Magazine, Civilian Job News*, and the *WSJ Career Journal*. She has also written for Military OneSource, ClearanceJobs, Military Money, the Army Wife Network, and the National Military Spouse Network.

She is a noted Powerhouse Military Spouse for the Military Spouse Corporate Career Network and currently serves as a panel expert for the National Military Spouse Network. She has been quoted as a subject matter expert on CareerBuilder.com and featured on Military Spouse Talk Radio.

You can follow Janet's timely tips and observations on Twitter at SmartJobChoices and Mil2CivGuide as well as subscribe to her newsletter for job-seeking military spouses by sending an email to JanetFarley@JanetFarley.com

Introduction

THE PROCESS OF finding and keeping a job or a career is not an easy one for anyone in today's volatile economy. Throw in the unusual challenges and obstacles that come with a life married to someone in the military and it can almost seem impossible at times.

Don't let the imposed challenges of tough economic times and the mobile military lifestyle get you down, though. Anyone, including you, can get a job or launch a career with a little logitivity.

Do You Have Logitivity?

Let me explain.

Admittedly, **logitivity** is not a real word but according to my ten-year old daughter it should be. She might have a point, particularly if you think of it as it applies to career-minded military spouses.

Logitivity = logic + creativity

It takes a healthy dose of both logical thinking and creativity to ferret out job opportunities or how those opportunities could potentially be created. It takes another dose of logitivity to get out there and convince an employer to hire you – and to go through that process time and time again.

Logitivity. Out of the mouths of babes...

The Military Spouse's Employment Guide: Smart Job Choices for Mobile Lifestyles wholeheartedly supports the concept of logitivity as a key ingredient in making smart job choices either on a stand-alone basis or as an integral part of a long-term career path.

Simply put, it's not enough for mobile military spouses living the camouflaged life to be qualified for a job. We have to be **creative** in our thinking, reaching **outside** the proverbial box for potential solutions. We've got to be willing to adjust fire along the way in order to secure employment and to do it every time the marching orders send us to a new duty station.

Who's in Control?

We know all too well that things don't always go our way. Change, no matter how sorely needed, is often slow in coming or somehow slightly off the mark.

We may not have control over those things around us, but we can control how we perceive the situation and deal with it. We have to if we're going to make any headway in our careers.

Succeeding in today's job market under the best of circumstances isn't easy.

The facts are clear. The nation's unemployment rate is higher than it has been in years and shows no sign of subsiding significantly anytime soon. Dollars, both within military communities and outside the main gates, are tight and will get tighter.

Succeeding in today's job market under the best of circumstances isn't easy. Succeeding in it, as a military spouse, requires know-how, courage, motivation, and perseverance.

Just for You

That is where *The Military Spouse's Employment Guide: Smart Job Choices for Mobile Lifestyles* comes in to serve you.

This book is targeted primarily to spouses who are new to the military lifestyle or to the workforce itself. It is also written for spouses who want to re-enter the workforce after being away from it for a period of time.

Spouses who already have well-established careers will also find helpful information here for themselves and for those they mentor along the way.

Finally, policymakers and family service providers will find the book a valuable resource as they formulate relevant policy and provide employment services to our military families near and far.

The Military Spouse's Employment Guide: Smart Job Choices for Mobile Lifestyles helps readers to accomplish the following:

- Think outside the box and effectively manage employment expectations
- Learn about smart job choices that can PCS easily
- Network effectively with others, on- and off-line
- Enhance marketability to get the attention of employers
- Create and revise resumes and cover letters
- Launch successful job search campaigns
- Confront and overcome the obstacles to employment imposed by a mobile military lifestyle

The book is divided into three main parts:

In **Part I, Smart Job Choices**, we look at the ever-present realities that come with a life married to the military today and we examine the potential solutions for dealing with them. We then take a closer look at specific industries and jobs that travel easily, making them smart job choices.

In **Part II, Smart Job Search Strategies**, you will find invaluable job search tools and techniques to help you land the position you want in today's competitive job market.

In **Part III, Smart Job Solutions for a Military Lifestyle**, you will find the answers to the toughest employment challenges that often confront military spouses.

It is my sincere hope that *The Military Spouse's Employment Guide: Smart Job Choices for Mobile Lifestyles* will be your go-to resource today and throughout your journey as a military spouse.

Janet Farley

PART I
Smart Job Choices

1

Military Lifestyle Realities Today

NO ONE HAS to tell you about it. You already know that being a military spouse is not an easy job on any level, be it personal or professional. On the clock and off, it is a life of continuing sacrifice and untold service without a uniform or a paycheck.

Our Challenges

Our work on the home front or in the workplace has always been a challenging one, more so in the last decade as our nation has been involved in major wars.

Looking at the bigger picture, it has been more than 10 years since the world forever changed on a cool, crisp September morning in 2001. It was then that a life of uncertainty, characteristic in military families, morphed into a life of uncertainty times 100.

Multiple and dangerous deployments have become the norm for many in uniform. Those who haven't deployed have nevertheless worked longer hours in support of world missions.

> **We can expect budgetary cuts and reorganizations to affect our community and long-term benefits.**

In between the deployments and the long hours, training requirements have seen our uniformed loved ones pack a bag and disappear from our lives for long stretches of time, leaving family members alone once again to manage the business of everyday life minus a mother, a father, or sometimes both.

The numbers from this past decade are discouraging. Over 6,000 service-members have died (Department of Defense Casualty Status Report, August 17, 2011) and the number of those wounded exceeds 43,000 (Wounded Warriors in Action Report, May 27, 2011). We may never know the true number of those experiencing post-traumatic stress disorder in or out of uniform.

To say that lives and minds, serving in or out of uniform, have been forever changed is a gross understatement. And, as always, continued change is imminent.

Without a doubt, more challenges are sure to follow for the military and our families in the coming days, months, and years as our nation works its way through the Great Recession. In short, we can expect budgetary cuts and reorganizations to affect our community and long-term benefits.

Clearly, the difficulties are many. The pressure is unmistakably on and, as always, military spouses will rise to the occasion. It's what we do.

You Know You're a Military Spouse When...

Despite many family and relocation challenges, military spouses manage to get by and thrive in this crazy life.

You know you're a military spouse when:

▶ ...Your packing skills are superior to those of the movers who show up on your doorstep on the average of every 2.9 years to haul your belongings off to your new duty station.

▶ ...You are far too practiced in saying goodbye to the one person you love the most. Between the last kiss and next one, you are left to hold everything together while life strangely stands still and marches on at the same time.

▶ ...You hold your breath while watching the evening news or scanning the daily headlines because there is always a connection to your life, near or far, and it's usually not a good one.

▶ ...You take the first steps to greet a new neighbor in the hopes that what goes around, comes around. You know what it feels like to be the new family on the street or in the stairwell.

▶ ...You are fiercely proud of your country and your spouse because you know not just anyone can do it. It takes more than a special person to live the life, putting country and mission first, with family falling somewhere behind. It takes a near saint to be married to someone like that. It takes a military spouse.

A Perfect Storm in the Making

It's not enough that our personal lives are full of extraordinary challenges. Our professional lives are full of them, too. More often than not, the two sets of challenges, personal and professional, create the conditions for a perfect storm of stress, uncertainty, and frustration in our lives.

> **Military orders send us to places where there are few job opportunities.**

It's easy to see how that can happen.

Military orders send us to places where there are few job opportunities or where employers are hesitant to hire someone who will move away after a couple years on the job. Why bother training them only to see them go? Never mind that anyone hired locally could leave the job just as easily.

Even if we are lucky enough to be stationed in an area where jobs are plentiful (or at least appear to be), we have other stressors to deal with as well:

- Surviving the PCS (Permanent Change of Station) move and getting everyone in the family adjusted.
- Having your spouse deploy, often multiple times, leaving you to operate solo.
- Increased military workloads that leave you on your own.
- Long childcare wait lists that prevent you from seeking employment.
- Continued lack of credentialing and licensing reciprocity nationwide.
- Funding fears on both Big Military levels and within your own wallet.
- Rise of compassion fatigue among our families.
- Never-ending uncertainty about the future.

As if the stress of being a military spouse in a time of war and a changed world isn't enough all by itself, sometimes the unthinkable happens. A loved one dies or is severely injured, changing our lives even further in ways we never ever imagined.

The Focus on Work

The perfect storm or not, we spouses choose to work – or we at least try our best to do so. For all the agony and ecstasy involved on any given day, the act of working offers you diverse opportunities that make it all worth it on one level or another.

Specifically, working enables you to:

- Have your own identity, apart from your spouse and the military lifestyle.
- Add to your ever-growing levels of self-esteem and professional confidence.
- Be part of a bigger picture, making a positive difference for others along the way.
- Pay your monthly bills or eliminate long-term debt.
- Accumulate brand-new debt to pay off as well.
- Help you afford things without accumulating debt in the first place.
- Put a college degree to work or fund a tuition bill for someone.
- Set a good, productive example for your children.
- Keep your skills from becoming obsolete in an ever-changing workplace.
- Avoid the stay-at-home spouse insanity that strikes on occasion.

Work matters to you and it should. Whether your reasons are intrinsic, financial, forced, or just because, work matters to you and it should. In this world, be it from 9 to 5 or whenever you are on the job, you are the sponsor. You get to make the choices. And you get to make them frequently…every time you PCS to a new duty station.

The Decisions Belong to You

While it can be hard to believe sometimes, you do call all the shots when it comes to your employment situation and you can choose to do anything.

You can choose to:

- Work in a job that pays well and brings you professional satisfaction.
- Volunteer in your community without a paycheck.
- Spend your time working on an advanced degree or certificate for the future.
- Work in the right job or a job for right now.
- Be self-employed.
- Live your life as a domestic goddess, forgoing paid employment altogether.

The choice is yours, although circumstances, usually not of your making, often get in the way.

You may not always get the job you want when you want it. It may not exist where you are stationed. Someone else may already hold that job, showing no signs of leaving anytime soon.

> **Smart job choices can be achieved in this military lifestyle despite the personal and professional challenges that come with being a military spouse.**

You may not be qualified for the job you want. Or you may be adequately qualified for it, applied for it, and interviewed for it, but another candidate may get the job offer.

You might be stationed someplace in the world where opportunities on the installation are few and working off the installation isn't even a legal option.

When circumstances get in your way, you may be forced to take a different direction for yourself professionally, maybe even one you never imagined before. Be open to the possibilities when that happens. You could end up with the best job you've ever had in your life. If not, at least you will know what you **don't** want to do in the future.

Smart job choices can be achieved in this military lifestyle despite the personal and professional challenges that come with being a military spouse.

The rest of this book will help you to make those choices for yourself.

2

Self-Assessment and Education

TOUGH TIMES AND tough situations require smart job decisions. Nobody wants to waste what precious time we have while being stationed somewhere we try to think of as "home" by making the wrong decisions.

It's not difficult to make smart employment-related decisions but it can be frustrating. Sometimes the choices put before us are very limited. For example, you may not want to choose between two offered jobs when neither is your first choice. If you want to work, you may have to suck it up and pick one anyway.

If you are making a smart job decision, you will pick the one that most closely fits with your skills, abilities, and interests. You also know that you can continue searching for a better job while being gainfully employed, taking comfort in the perverse reality that it is easier to get a new job when you already have one.

It's not exactly a news flash that we don't always get what we want professionally.

We can come closer to getting what we want, closer to making the right decision along the way, if we periodically take the time to reassess where we are in terms of our skills, where we want to be, and how we might actually get there.

American journalist Sydney Harris said, "Ninety percent of the world's woes come from people not knowing themselves, their abilities, their frailties, and even their real virtues. Most of us go almost all the way through life as complete strangers to ourselves."

Don't be a complete stranger to yourself.

Skills Check: Getting to Know All About You

What skills do you have that you can clearly identify? You need to know all about them, including the ones you like to use and the ones you don't, if you are ever going to convince an employer to hire you because of your skills.

The next few pages give you the opportunity to reassess your self-management, transferable or functional, and technical skills. As you go through each of the exercises, you will be asked to **identify the top five skills** that:

- are your strongest
- you like to use the most
- you least like using
- you don't have but want to obtain

Yes. It's a bit of pain to do it. Do it anyway.

Self-Management Skills

Self-management skills are those skills that you bring to the wonderful world of work as a person in general. They represent your signature style, if you will. Employers want to score a hiring trifecta by employing you. They want you to be able to do the job, to be willing to do the job, and they want you to fit in with everyone else at work.

Here is an extensive list of common self-management skills. Read over the list briefly at first and then get down to the hard work of identifying your top fives in the spaces provided on the next pages.

Commonly Noted Self-Management Skills

Accurate	Analytical	Careful
Active	Artistic	Caring
Adaptable	Assertive	Cautious
Adventurous	Bold	Charismatic
Affectionate	Broad-minded	Charming
Aggressive	Calm	Cheerful
Alert	Candid	Clear-headed
Ambitious	Capable	Clever

Competent	Firm	Natural
Competitive	Flexible	Non-judgmental
Concerned	Forceful	Obliging
Concise	Frank	Open-minded
Confident	Friendly	Opportunistic
Conscientious	Frugal	Optimistic
Conservative	Generous	Organized
Considerate	Gentle	Original
Consistent	Genuine	Patient
Cooperative	Goal-oriented	Perfectionist
Courageous	Good-natured	Persevering
Creative	Hardworking	Precise
Curious	Healthy	Productive
Daring	Helpful	Progressive
Decisive	Honest	Prudent
Dedicated	Humorous	Punctual
Deliberate	Idealistic	Quick-study
Dependable	Imaginative	Quiet
Detail-oriented	Independent	Realistic
Determined	Individualistic	Reasonable
Dignified	Industrious	Reflective
Diligent	Informal	Reliable
Direct	Ingenious	Resourceful
Disciplined	Innovative	Responsible
Discreet	Intellectual	Risk-taker
Dominant	Intelligent	Secure
Eager	Intuitive	Self-confident
Easygoing	Likable	Self-motivated
Efficient	Logical	Sensible
Emotional	Loyal	Sensitive
Energetic	Mature	Serious
Enterprising	Methodical	Sharp-witted
Enthusiastic	Meticulous	Sincere
Factual	Mild-mannered	Spunky
Fair-minded	Modest	Stable

Strong	Tenacious	Verbal
Strong-minded	Thorough	Versatile
Strong-willed	Thoughtful	Warm
Sympathetic	Tolerant	Willingness
Tactful	Tough	Wise
Talented	Trustworthy	Witty
Teachable	Understanding	

Self-Management Skills Analysis

My top five strongest skills are:

1. _____
2. _____
3. _____
4. _____
5. _____

The top five skills I have that I like to use the most:

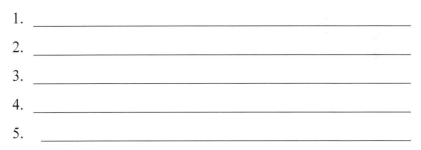

1. _____
2. _____
3. _____
4. _____
5. _____

The top five skills I have that I dislike using the most:

1. _____
2. _____
3. _____
4. _____
5. _____

The top five skills I don't have now but want to obtain in the future:

1. _____

2. _____

3. _____

4. _____

5. _____

Transferable or Functional Skills

Transferable or functional skills are your go-to skills that enable you to work across industries. What they lack in specificity, they more than make up for in practicality. They are abilities that you have in one area that can be applied in other areas as well.

Think of them as a bridge that can lead to new employment opportunities when you need them to do so. They often are associated with such broad-brush stroke headings as communication skills, organizational planning, management and leadership skills, and basic interpersonal skills.

Here is yet another extensive list of words for you to consider. This time, however, the list reflects common transferrable or functional skills. Just as you did in the previous exercise, read over the list briefly at first. Then pick out your list of top fives again at the end, where space is provided.

Commonly Noted Transferable/Functional Skills

Adjust	Calculate	Consult
Advise	Care for	Cook
Alter	Classify	Coordinate
Analyze	Compare	Copy
Arrange	Compile	Create
Assess	Compose	Decorate
Assist	Compute	Demonstrate
Blend	Conceptualize	Diagnose
Budget	Construct	Direct

Drive	Investigate	Record
Edit	Learn	Refill
Entertain	Listen	Regulate
Evaluate	Manage	Repair
Examine	Manipulate	Report
Follow up	Measure	Sell
Formulate	Mix	Serve
Guide	Motivate	Service
Handle	Negotiate	Sew
Improvise	Network	Sort
Include	Operate	Supervise
Influence	Paint	Synthesize
Inform	Persuade	Teach
Insert	Plan	Test
Install	Post data	Theorize
Instruct	Problem solve	Transcribe
Interview	Publicize	Type
Invent	Read	Write

Transferable/Functional Skills Analysis

My top five strongest skills are:

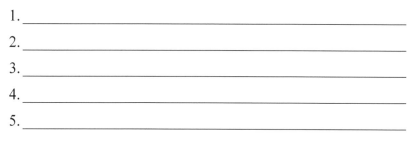

1. _____

2. _____

3. _____

4. _____

5. _____

The top five skills I have that I like to use the most:

1. _____

2. _____

3. _____

4. _____

5. _____

The top five skills I have that I dislike using the most:

1. _____

2. _____

3. _____

4. _____

5. _____

The top five skills I don't have now but want to obtain in the future:

1. _____

2. _____

3. _____

4. _____

5. _____

Technical Skills

Your self-management and transferable skills show the world how you handle yourself and what you can do across the job spectrum. Your technical skills, on the other hand, represent the more hardcore work-specific talents you possess that are required to do a job or a task.

For example, your technical skills could be a proficiency you have in operating a particular software program or the knowledge of a foreign language necessary to communicate with international customers. Consider also the specific licenses or certifications you possess that are required to do a particular job.

Think about all the jobs you have had in the past. What technical skills did you need to have in order to accomplish the tasks at hand?

Technical Skills Analysis

My top five strongest skills are:

1. _____
2. _____
3. _____
4. _____
5. _____

The top five skills I have that I like to use the most:

1. _____
2. _____
3. _____
4. _____
5. _____

The top five skills I have that I dislike using the most:

1. _____
2. _____
3. _____
4. _____
5. _____

The top five skills I don't have now but want to obtain in the future:

1. _____
2. _____
3. _____
4. _____
5. _____

Beyond the Skills: What Matters to You?

So you've taken the important time to put a name to your skills. Now what?

Carry your hard work to the next step and analyze why you filled in the blanks the way you did.

- Why do you like using some skills over others?
- What is it about using them that brings you professional satisfaction?
- How are you going to get those skills you don't have now, but want to obtain?

Consider writing your thoughts down in a journal you can call your very own **Smart Job Choices Journal**. Writing your thoughts down and brainstorming potential paths can help you focus better on the subject. It can bring you an inner clarity and peace, enabling you to get to know yourself better.

It can help you make smart job decisions when there are decisions to be made.

And, frankly, it's cheaper than paying a therapist.

If all this inner analysis leaves you wanting to learn more about your skills, preferences, and abilities, or if you need additional assistance to help you figure out what to do with the information, consider talking to a career counselor in person or over the phone.

There are a number of interest inventories or skill assessment tools that might provide you with more answers. A career counselor can tell you more about them, administer them to you, and help you understand their results.

You can check out **career assessment websites**. Some allow you to do a free self-assessment. Some websites to get you started:

www.careerpath.com
www.careertest.net
www.assessment.com
www.careerkey.com
www.livecareer.com/free-online-career-assessment-test

In addition, you may want to get a copy of this book: *Everything Career Tests Book*. It can be ordered from Impact Publications (see the order form at the end of this book). A description of it is given on Impact's website: www.impactpublications.com.

For **free career counseling**, visit or call:

- a career counselor at the nearest military education center
- a Military OneSource consultant at 1-800-342-9647
- a career counselor from a nearby college or university career center
- the employment readiness program manager at the nearby military family support center
- the job search specialist at the transition assistance center (TAP) if you are eligible to use it

There are also a number of excellent career coaches, some of whom have military spouse-specific expertise, who can assist you for a reasonable fee. See page 167 in the Go-To Resources section.

One thing seems certain: you don't want to waste your time doing something that doesn't matter to you in some important way. A decent-sized paycheck can be your main motivation for doing what you do. Or maybe it is the job itself that matters the most, giving you something that money can't exactly buy.

Whatever your personal reasons for doing what you do professionally, understand them clearly and continue to be true to them.

The Case for Higher Education and Continued Training

Your climb to employment success may ultimately crash and burn unless you nurture it along in the form of education and/or continued job training.

You need only refer back to your top-five lists of skills you don't have but want to obtain to grasp the importance of continued education and training.

If you're ready to think about the topic in more detail now, you should remember one hard truth before going any further:

▶ **You can't depend on anyone else to manage your continued professional development activities for you. You have to do it yourself, solo ops. You have the biggest investment in it.**

Your employer, your spouse, and even your mother may care a great deal about you, but the responsibility for getting and keeping yourself marketable through education and training is completely up to you.

And for all the time, dollars, and postponed plans in your life, it is worth it.

Studies have proven time and time again that whatever education you have pays off. It is the ticket leading you to a better job, a bigger paycheck, and increased opportunities for job enhancement and career advancement.

Here are the estimated average lifetime earnings by education level, if you need further convincing:

High school dropouts	$1,198,447
High school graduates	1,767,025
Some college	2,239,548
Associate degree	2,254,765
Bachelor's degree	3,380,060
Master's degree	3,837,239
Professional degree	4,650,588
PhD	4,029,948

Source: *Projections of Jobs and Education Requirements Through 2018*, June 2010. Authors: Carnevale, Smith and Strohl from Georgetown University's Center on Education and the Workforce.

Clearly, it pays to have a college degree. A formal academic education, however, isn't the only way to achieve higher earnings and better opportunities.

You can also enhance your marketability through participation in employer-sponsored training programs, by obtaining industry certifications and/or licenses, or by participating in and completing an accredited apprenticeship program. You can also do it through self-directed study and volunteering.

There are no limits on how you can better yourself unless you've imposed them.

Financing Education

Your mind may be in the right place, but perhaps your wallet isn't quite on board with the program yet. It's no secret that higher education and continued training can cost big bucks and finding the money to pay for them is no fun at all.

Maybe, just maybe, the fun happens when you get someone else to pick up all or part of the tab for your educational endeavors.

If you're interested in doing that, then let's look at some of the ways to avoid long-term debt as you pursue a better education.

▶ In-State Tuition Benefits

Because of the Higher Education Act, since July 1, 2009, military members, spouses, and their college-aged children have been guaranteed in-state tuition at public colleges and universities in the state where they reside or are permanently stationed. Before the Act was approved by Congress, many states offered the in-state tuition benefit while the military family member resided in the state, but some did not allow that rate to continue once a military family relocated due to orders. Now the nice rate continues and there is often a big difference between in- and out-of-state tuition rates.

▶ Post-9/11 GI Bill Transferability

You may be able to have your servicemember spouse's unused educational benefits transferred to you. There are a number of eligibility conditions and rules that you may be subject to in order to make that happen. You can read all about them on the Veterans Administration webpage dedicated to the GI Bill: http://gibill.va.gov.

▶ Scholarships

Scholarships are financial awards given to students by colleges, universities, or other organizations. You may qualify for them based on such factors as:

- past academic achievements (merit-based scholarships)
- unique abilities
- ethnicity and/or religious background
- being a military spouse
- being married to a disabled servicemember
- being a widow/widower of a servicemember killed during military service

If you apply for and receive a scholarship, you may be required to maintain a specific grade point average or else pay back the award. Each scholarship may have its own set of strings attached. You just have to read the fine print carefully to determine any restrictions or limitations. Scholarships targeted specifically to military spouses include:

- The Joanne Holbrook Patton Military Scholarship
- Air Force Association Spouse Scholarship
- Armed Forces Communications & Electronics Association (AFCEA) Educational Foundation
- University of Maryland Spouse Scholarships
- Navy Supply Corps Foundation Scholarship Program
- Pat Tillman Military Scholarships
- Wings Over American Scholarship Foundation
- Folds of Honor Funds Scholarships

▶ **Grants and Fellowships**

Grants and fellowships are wonderfully free gifts of money usually offered by the federal government, colleges, universities, and public or private organizations and corporations.

Similar to scholarships, grants are awarded based on a variety of criteria such as financial need, academic achievements, ethnicity, and religious background. To research potential grant sources, visit the U.S. Department of Education (www.ed.gov) and click on the *Funding* link.

Examples of current federally funded grants include:

- The Federal Pell Grant
- The Federal Supplemental Education Opportunity Grant (FSEOG)
- TEACH Grant
- FINRA Foundation Military Spouse Fellowship Program

▶ **My Career Advancement Account (MyCAA)**

The MyCAA program, ambitiously launched in 2007 to benefit all military spouses, has since been scaled back significantly to accommodate spouses of junior servicemembers who are pursuing associate degrees, certificates, or licensure programs. It is still a good deal offering a $4,000 maximum benefit for those who are eligible.

The program is currently open to spouses of active duty Army, Navy, Air Force, or Marine servicemembers in the pay grades E1-E5, W1-W2, and O1-O2. If you are a military spouse of a National Guard and/or AGR member, your sponsor must be on federal Title 10 active duty orders as reported in DEERS in order for you take advantage of MyCAA.

Learn more about the program by contacting Military OneSource at 1-800-273-8255 or visiting their website: www.militaryonesource.mil.

▶ **Work-Study Programs**

In a work-study program, you work for an organization and, in return, receive money for your education. You can find out about potential work-study programs through the college you are attending or thinking about attending. Many such programs are sponsored by the federal and state governments and are designed to promote community service and work related to the area of study.

For example, the Veterans Administration (VA) has a work-study allowance available to veterans who are training under specific VA benefit programs. If you are also a veteran in addition to being a military spouse now, you may qualify. Other family members may also be eligible. Check with the VA (www.va.gov) for more details.

▶ **Low or No Interest Loans**

Go for any free money you can get your hands on first, but don't rule out reasonable education loans either. To learn about the different types of student loans, visit the Free Application for Federal Student Aid at www.fafsa.ed.gov. Another helpful site full of good information is The Smart Student Guide to Financial Aid at www. finaid.org. Examples of federal student loans today include:

- Stafford Loans
- Perkins Loans
- PLUS Loans for Parents
- PLUS Loans for Graduate and Professional Students

■ Military Relief Societies

All the service branches offer military spouse educational assistance as well. Each branch may have specific criteria, subject to change from year to year, for obtaining the financial aid. For more information about spouse scholarship and financial aid programs, see:

- Army Emergency Relief (AER): www.aerhq.org/education.asp
  - AER scholarships are considered grants.
- Navy and Marine Corps Relief Society: www.nmcrs.org/education
  - Offers scholarship and low interest loans based on financial need.
- Air Force Aid Society: www.afas.org/education
  - Offers Arnold Ed grants and Spouse Tuition Assistance Program (STAP).
- Coast Guard Mutual Assistance (CGMA): www.cgmahq.org/programs/education
  - Offers various educational grant and loan programs.

▶ Employer Tuition Reimbursement Benefits

Your current employer may offer to pick up the tab for a portion of your tuition bill. After all, your newly acquired knowledge and expertise may benefit the company as well. Check your employment contract to see if you have these benefits, or contact your human resources department for more information. Usually, you will have to pay for your tuition up-front and are reimbursed the money or a portion of it after presenting proof of a passing grade.

▶ **Employer Sponsored Training**

In addition to employer tuition reimbursement plans, the company you work for could also be an excellent source of professional development training opportunities. If you are not sure of the potential opportunities, ask your supervisor or human resources representative about the possibilities.

For more information about potential funding sources:

- Visit your military installation's education office or your college's career services office and speak with a career counselor.
- Call Military OneSource at 1-800-342-9647 for more information.

Buyer Beware: If It Sounds Too Good to be True...

You can buy anything these days, including your credentials by following these enticing but fraudulent headlines:

- "Get an Accredited College Degree in 5 Days!"
- "Buy an online degree on the basis of your life experiences"
- "Instant Degrees On-line Here!"
- "Buy an Accredited College Degree in 7 Days – No Exams, Fees or Studying."

There are an ever-increasing number of diploma mills posing as reputable learning institutions that will gladly confer a college degree upon you or award you with a shiny certificate. No hard work required on your part. All you have to do is pay for it.

Being a savvy spouse, you know a scam when you see one, and there are plenty of them out there today.

The Federal Trade Commission (FTC) is pretty savvy as well, and they encourage you to be suspicious too if these conditions exist:

- You don't have to study or take exams.
- You don't have to attend classes online or in person. Instead, you "earn" a degree based on your life experiences.
- You pay for a whole degree itself rather than for a credit, course, or semester.

- You don't have to wait long to receive your diploma in the mail.
- You find yourself being pressured via aggressive sales tactics, whether through online advertising, newspapers, magazines, or in person.
- You learn about a school through spam or pop-ups on your computer.

Earning a valid degree or professional certification from an accredited school or institution takes tuition dollars, your precious time, long-term dedication, and lots of hard work. There are no shortcuts.

3

Smart Mobile Job Choices

YOU'VE NO DOUBT heard the tired but true military spouse employment mantra before: **Have job, will travel**.

In theory, it should work without a hitch. In reality, it doesn't always. Something always pops up to complicate the matter. Regardless, the concept is solid and it remains the best solution for the moment.

In Focus: Smart Jobs for You to Consider

In the previous chapter you analyzed your **skills**. You know what you like to do, what you don't like to do, and what you want to learn how to do. You've thought about the importance of education and training and how you might make your goals of experiencing them a reality.

Now, we're going to focus on **specific jobs** that do travel well and may fit in with your own mobile lifestyle. It is not a complete list by any means. The point of having it here is to encourage you to think of the mobile employment possibilities that could work for you.

Each entry lists:

- A smart job choice selected by the author
- A range of reported average salaries
- A short commentary about the smart job of choice
- A list of jobs related to the one highlighted to give you even more ideas
- Where you can go to get more career information about the job

Some salary data and job descriptions were adapted from the latest *Occupation Outlook Handbook* (www.bls.gov/oco). The newest editions should be available online for you to learn even more about the jobs mentioned here.

23

Sprinkled throughout the descriptions, you will find words of wisdom from fellow military spouses who work in smart jobs and have volunteered to share their valuable insights with you. You will find them under the title "A Smart Job Voice of Experience."

Finally, a "Short List of Other Smart Job Choices" is provided for you at the end of the chapter, on pages 49-50.

CONSULTANT

National Average Salary: Hourly Rates of $11.64 – $62.69

Comments: It is said that those who can't do, teach. Maybe those who can't work, consult. (Ba-da-bing.)

In any event, consulting is alive and well and reaches across just about every industry, with information being the hot commodity. The job outlook is terrific, with employment projected to increase a whopping 83% through 2018. Educationally speaking, consultants generally have a bachelor's degree or higher. Many consultants are self-employed and contract out their services while others work as employees of an organization.

This is clearly an attractive option for you if you have expertise that others may be interested in having and are willing to pay you for sharing. Think about past jobs you've had and how you could potentially parlay them into a consulting gig. Any subject area is game for being marketed.

Where They Work:

Consultants working for a company or individual clients may work on or off site in virtually any industry. They may have a dedicated office or they may work out of their home.

Related Jobs:

- Accountant and Auditor
- Administrative Service Manager/
- Assistant
- Advertising Manager
- Computer Scientist
- Computer Technician/Manager
- Designer
- Economist
- Engineer
- Financial Manager
- Lawyer
- Management Analyst

For More Information:

- Association of Management Consulting Firms
  www.amcf.org
- Institute of Management Consultants USA
  www.imcusa.org
- Professional and Technical Consultants Association (PATCA)
  www.patca.org
- National Business Association (NBA)
  www.nationalbusiness.org
- SCORE: For the Life of Your Business
  www.score.org

PERSONAL FINANCIAL ADVISOR

National Average Salary: $46,390 – $119,290

Comments: If Warren Buffet is your American Idol and the CNN Money website your first stop every morning with a cup of coffee, then you may be a candidate for job within the financial services industry.

Personal financial advisors, generally speaking, have strong math, analytical, and interpersonal skills. They use these sharp mental powers to help others assess their financial needs on both a short- and long-term basis. In the process, they assist them with investments, tax laws, and insurance issues.

Many advisors are self-employed and rely on a solid database of repeat clients. This can be a smart job choice for military spouses whose wide-ranging contacts list (aka potential client base) can be long and far-reaching thanks to multiple PCS moves. (Just how long is your holiday card list?) Closely akin to the advisor is the financial counselor, who doesn't sell products but, rather, provides counseling and education services.

This is a great job for military spouses because everyone these days can use a little more financial education and good advice, including our military communities. The Financial Industry Regulatory Authority, Inc. (FINRA) believes this too and has consequently established the FINRA Foundation Military Spouse Fellowship Program. The fellowship pays for selected spouses annually to earn the Accredited Financial Counselor® designation.

For more information, visit Save and Invest (www.saveandinvest.org).

Where They Work:

Many financial advisors work independently from their own offices or even from home. Others may work for a larger firm or as the independent owner of a national franchise such as Edward Jones or Met Life. Some advisors try to expand their client base by teaching evening classes at colleges or business schools or by offering seminars where they not only teach but recruit clients as well.

Related Jobs:

- Accountant and Auditor
- Actuary
- Budget Analyst
- Financial Manager
- Financial Analyst
- Insurance Sales Agent
- Insurance Underwriter
- Real Estate Broker and Sales Agent
- Securities Sales Agent
- Financial Sales Agent

For More Information:

- Financial Industry Regulatory Authority (FINRA)
  www.finra.org
- Certified Financial Planner Board of Standards
  www.cfp.net
- Financial Planning Association
  www.fpanet.org
- National Association of Personal Financial Advisors (NAPFA)
  www.napfa.org
- International Association of Registered Financial Consultants
  www.iarfc.org

A Smart Job Voice of Experience

FINANCIAL COUNSELOR ASSISTS MILITARY FAMILIES

Financial counselors have a unique opportunity to assist service members and their families in the complex process of improving their financial situation.

This very customer-service oriented profession is focused on advising and assisting clients in the process of overcoming financial indebtedness and helping them identify and modify ineffective money management behaviors.

Equally important, financial counselors can guide clients through financial challenges and help them develop successful strategies to achieve their financial goals.

Financial advisers can also assist clients in planning and arranging their financial affairs. This might include advising clients on financial risk management tools, and helping them look toward the future, by addressing savings and retirement planning, and the importance of estate planning.

With the global nature of today's lifestyle, clients and financial counselors don't even need to be in the same time zone.

This very portable career is really ideal for the military spouse who likes to work independently, either in person, online, or over the telephone. And the professional associations, both AFCPE.com and NAPFA.com, provide outstanding conferences, and educational webinars and seminars designed to help a professional obtain and maintain their professional certifications, again, either in person or through online opportunities.

Jacquelyn Nasca, MS
Military Spouse and Retired Personnel Officer
www.FocusOnYourMoney.com

GRAPHIC DESIGNER

National Average Salary: $ 32,600 – $56,620

Comments: Are they artists, engineers, Walt Disney World wannabes, or grown-up children playing with computer-controlled crayons? Who knows? Without them, however, life would certainly be less visually appealing.

Graphic designers do with visuals what writers do with words. They plan, analyze, and create visual solutions to communicate ideas, and they do it in print and electronic media using color, type, illustration, photography, animation, and other print and layout techniques. Designers may create solutions to specific problems, produce promotional materials, or devise industry signage.

If you have the abilities needed to work in this job, you may find it a smart and portable job choice. Jobs are expected to grow 13% and competition will be tough for those jobs. Those having web design and animation experience are predicted to have the best opportunities.

Within the military community, you are likely to find paid job opportunities at the Public Affairs Office or the Morale, Welfare and Recreation facilities and volunteer opportunities everywhere else.

Everyone who wants his "death by PowerPoint" slideshow presentation to be the best wants a good graphic designer.

Where They Work:

The work settings of graphic designers can vary. They may work in their own offices or in the offices of their customers. They can find jobs within any industry for the most part, but advertising, publishing, and design firms are the big areas. Some successful designers eventually move on to teaching their trade at design schools or in colleges and universities.

Related Jobs:

- Artist
- Industrial Designer
- Fashion Designer
- Floral Designer
- Interior Designer
- Computer Software Engineer
- Desktop Publisher
- Advertising Manager
- Public Relations Manager
- Photographer
- Writer and Editor

For More Information:

- National Association of Schools of Art and Design
  http://nasad.arts-accredit.org
- American Institute of Graphic Arts
  www.aiga.org
- Art Directors Club
  www.adcglobal.org
- International Council of Graphic Design Associations
  www.icograda.org
- American Association of Advertising Agencies
  www.aaaa.org

A Smart Job Voice of Experience

CAPTURING THE MOMENT AS WELL AS A CAREER

Photography is something I stumbled into and fell deeply in love with. A personal quest to catalogue the intimate moments of my own family has grown into a passion for capturing life moments for others.

As a unique combination of science and art, this career offers both a constant learning curve and an opportunity to create a personal flexible schedule. It's quickly becoming a popular mobile career choice for military spouses, too.

Relocating to a new community can create significant challenges as a photographer. You have to re-establish local client connections and obtain any required business approvals and licenses. Plus, you have to spend time discovering where new shooting locations are in your area and you have to set up a whole new studio environment.

Luckily, in today's age of social media, online networking and searching for resources can begin the moment new PCS orders are cut.

If you are interested in pursuing photography, reach out to professionals in your local community or find a local photo walk club for enthusiasts to participate in and learn.

Much like anything in military life, your career is what you make of it. Success isn't always measured in dollars – but rather the richness that comes with experiences and friendships, which will enhance our lives.

Be passionate. Enjoy yourself. Be unique. Create something useful. And remember to give back to those just beginning their journey!

Ann Marie Detavernier
Army Spouse and Photographer
www.household6diva.com

INTERIOR DESIGNER

National Average Salary: $ 34,620 – $61,880

Comments: They beautify our world in the name of feng shui, increased sales, and productivity.

Interior designers plan the interior spaces of homes, businesses, shopping malls, theaters, restaurants, hotels, hospitals, and any other place you can imagine. Working closely with customers, they focus not only on the decorating itself but also on the architectural detailing as well.

Designers must be able to read blueprints, understand building and fire codes, and know how to make places accessible for those with disabilities. Expertise using computer-aided software design is a plus. Some states may require an associate or bachelor's degree or a state license to work as an interior designer.

The job outlook through 2018 is positive, with opportunities expected to grow at about 19%. An interesting prediction is that interior designers may find ample work within the healthcare industry as aging boomers move into live-in facilities.

Interior design is a smart job choice for military spouses. After all, who could possibly know more about decorating a place than someone who has lived in plenty of them?

Where They Work:

As noted above, many interior designers work in individual homes, businesses, shopping centers, entertainment venues, dining establishments, schools, healthcare facilities, and within the hospitality industry. Many work out of their own office or on site of a client or employer. In any event, interior designers aren't usually found sitting at their desk for a standard eight-hour day. They are out and about, beautifying the world for the rest of us.

Related Jobs:

- Architect
- Artist
- Commercial and Industrial Designer
- Fashion Designer
- Floral Designer
- Graphic Designer
- Landscape Architect

For More Information:

- American Society of Interior Designers
  www.asid.org

- Council for Interior Design Accreditation
  www.accredit-id.org

- National Council for Interior Design Qualification
  www.ncidq.org

- International Interior Design Association
  www.iida.org
- Interior Design Society
  www.interiordesignsociety.org

A Smart Job Voice of Experience

INTERIOR DECORATOR GETS PAID FOR SHOPPING

I have always loved shopping, and now I get paid to do it for others!

As a self-employed interior decorator, I help my clients get the most out of their environments. The scope of my projects is entirely determined by the needs of my clients. One day, you could find me poring over design magazines, drafting floor plans, visiting showrooms to look at furniture, and fabric samples, or visiting with clients. The next day I might be meeting with contractors, coordinating deliveries, keeping track of orders and payments, or putting together presentations for multiple clients.

Being the boss, I can make my own hours and can take on as much or as little work as I think I can handle at any given time. I chose to be an interior decorator because it was a good fit with my skills and past work experiences. The job also travels well and that helps when you're married to a Marine. Wherever we are stationed, there are people who need help with decorating, and there are design centers and furniture stores nationwide. I can choose to either work for myself or for another employer where I can learn even more about the business while having a steady income and set schedule.

If you plan to go into the interior decorating business for yourself, check with your local authorities regarding legal requirements specific to your city or state. You will probably need a resale certificate and a business license. Industry certifications aren't required but can give you a lot of credibility with customers. Interior decorating really is the perfect career choice for me. I can take my career with me anywhere I go.

Deb Milstein
Marine Corps Spouse, Certified Interior Decorator
Household Six Interiors

LIFE COACH

National Average Salary: $100 – $150 per hour

Comments: They may not have all the answers you seek to life's burning questions, but they might be able to help you get to those answers yourself.

According to the Institute of Life Coaching, this relatively new career field helps those who are already successful to a certain degree become even more successful by helping them to realize their full potential. In the process, they guide clients in designing a strategy for overcoming any obstacles that stand in the way of achieving success.

Life coaches, important to note, are not therapists, consultants, or counselors. They focus on an individual's strengths, purpose, and goals with an eye to the future rather than the past. Some coaches specialize in specific life areas such as relationships, wellness, and business.

To work as a life coach, you should feel comfortable in your own skin first and have the ability to work independently. Excellent communication and people skills are a must, as is the desire to help others attain their goals. Strong business skills are also useful, as many coaches are self-employed, working on a consulting basis.

Certification is not required to work as a life coach, but many who claim the job title do maintain one or more credentials. There are a number of different organizations that offer them.

Where They Work:

Many life coaches are self-employed and may work out of their own offices or homes. Some work virtually online with their clients or over the telephone, making this a smart job choice for mobile spouses.

Related Jobs:

- Financial Empowerment Coach
- Career or Job Coach
- Live-In Life Skills Coach
- Fitness and Nutrition Coach
- Wellness Coach
- Health and Social Services
- Assistant

For More Information:

- The Institute for Life Coach Training
  www.lifecoachtraining.com
- Institute for Professional Excellence in Coaching
  www.ipeccoaching.com
- International Coach Federation (ICF)
  www.coachfederation.org
- International Association of Coaching
  www.certifiedcoach.org
- Coach Inc
  www.coachinc.com
- Coach U
  www.coachu.com
- Coach Training Institute (CTI)
  www.thecoaches.com

MEDICAL TRANSCRIPTIONIST

National Average Salary: $13.02 – $18.55 per hour

Comments: You've seen your military medical records before. How much of what's in those pages can you actually understand? If you can decipher most of it, you might have a knack for becoming a medical transcriptionist.

Medical transcriptionists listen to dictated recordings made by healthcare professionals and transcribe them into medical reports, correspondence, and other administrative materials. Using a headset and a foot pedal to pause the recordings as needed, transcriptionists create readable documents that become a part of a patient's permanent medical file.

Those who work in this job must understand medical terminology, anatomy and physiology, diagnostic procedures, pharmacology and treatment assessments. They must have excellent English grammar skills. Transcriptionists require good visual and auditory abilities and excellent listening skills. They must possess excellent keyboarding skills and the ability to work for long hours with a high level of concentration.

Formal accreditation for working in this career is not required. Transcriptionists earning the bigger bucks, however, are Certified Medical Transcriptionists (CMTs). To be eligible to take the CMT exam, you must first successfully complete two years of practical work experience as a medical transcriptionist.

Those who have recently graduated from a medical transcription educational program but have fewer than two years of work experience may become Registered Medical Transcriptionists (RMTs). The Association for Healthcare Documentation Integrity (AHDI) awards the voluntary designations.

Where They Work:

Medical transcriptionists work in hospitals, private practices, laboratories, medical libraries, and government healthcare facilities. Some work in offices dedicated to providing medical transcription services while others telecommute from home, making this a highly portable job prospect for spouses.

Related Jobs:

- Medical Records Technician
- Medical Assistant
- Secretary
- Administrative Assistant
- Court Reporter

For More Information:

- Medical Transcriptionist
  www.medicaltranscriptionist.org
- Association for Healthcare Documentation Integrity (AHDI)
  www.ahdionline.org (Note: AHDI was formerly known as the American Association for Medical Transcription)
- Meditec
  www.meditec.com
- Clinical Documentation Industry Association (CDIA)
  www.mtia.com
- HIMSS: Transforming Healthcare Through IT
  www.himss.org

PARALEGAL

National Average Salary: $36,080 – $59,310

Comments: Paralegals do the all-important grunt work behind the court-room scenes, including helping the lawyers prepare for closings, hearings, trials, and meetings. They investigate the facts of a case and identify the relevant and applicable laws, judicial decisions, and legal articles needed to build the cases. Essentially, they do it all except set legal fees, give legal advice, and present cases in court.

As you might guess, having a strong attention to detail is important. Para-legals work closely with the public and having good people and com-munication skills is key. Additionally, paralegals are expected, like their attorney counterparts, to uphold the ethical standards that theoretically exist in the legal profession. Depending on who is your employer, you may work a sane 40 hours a week or not. Often, the closer a case gets to court, the more intense the work schedule. Come on. You've watched "Law and Order." You know how it works.

In the larger organizations, area specialization is common. You might find these savvy assistants working solely in areas such as litigation, personal injury, corporate law, criminal law, employee benefits, bankruptcy, or other legal areas. In smaller firms, paralegals may do a little of everything – a proverbial jack of all trades.

You can become a paralegal in several different ways. Attending a community college that offers a paralegal program leading to an associate's degree is the most common route, according to the U.S. Bureau of Labor Statistics. Those who already have a degree, however, may earn a certificate in paralegal studies. Still others attend colleges or universities that offer programs, or they receive on the job training in the field.

It is not necessary to have a certification to work as a paralegal. Those who do have one, however, are more marketable and earn a better salary. Different organizations offer their own versions of certifications. Some of the more recognized certifications include the Certified Legal Assistant (CLA) or Certified Paralegal (CP) credential offered by the National Association of Legal Assistants. The American Alliance of Paralegals, Inc. offers the American Alliance Certified Paralegal (AACP) credential. The

National Federation of Paralegal Associations (NFPA) offers the Registered Paralegal (RP) designation.

Where They Work:

If you are paralegal, you might work in a law firm, a corporate legal department, or a government office.

Related Jobs:

- Law Clerk
- Claims Adjuster
- Examiner
- Investigator
- Title Examiner
- Abstractor
- Researcher

For More Information:

- National Association of Legal Assistants (NALA)
  www.nala.org
- The American Alliance of Paralegals, Inc.
  www.aapipara.org
- National Federation of Paralegal Associations (NFPA)
  www.paralegals.org
- Paralegal Degree Information
  www.paralegaldegreeinfo.com
- American Bar Association: Getting Legal with Paralegals (A Look at State Regulations)
  http://apps.americanbar.org/buslaw/blt/2007-01-02/durgin.shtml
- American Bar Association (homepage)
  www.americanbar.org

PERSONAL TRAINER

National Average Salary: $19,610 – $44,420 median average

Comments: If physical fitness is one of your strengths and you enjoy helping others attain their physical strength and endurance goals, then you might enjoy working as a personal trainer.

Trainers are usually certified professionals who often specialize in one or more areas and assist clients in assessing and achieving their specific fitness goals. They may work on a one-on-one with clients or in groups.

Certifications are not always required to do the job, but having one or more makes you a better candidate for employment.

Demand for personal trainers is expected to increase 29% over the next decade, making the job one that isn't going away anytime soon and one that is quite military spouse friendly. Personal training is a job that can be done on full or part time basis, making it a wonderfully flexible occupation.

Where They Work:

Personal trainers can be found working in many different settings that include military gyms, health clubs, hospitals, universities, resorts, and even private homes.

Related Jobs:

- Athlete
- Coach
- Dietitian
- Nutritionist
- Physical Therapist
- Recreation Worker
- Wellness Coach

For More Information:

- American College of Sports Medicine
  www.acsm.org
- American Council on Exercise
  www.acefitness.org
- National Academy of Sports Medicine
  www.nasm.org
- NSCA Certification Commission
  www.nsca-cc.org
- IDEA Health and Fitness Association
  www.ideafit.com

A Smart Job Voice of Experience

HAVING IT ALL AND HELPING OTHERS TO DO THE SAME

As a professional coach, I get to do something I love, and balance that with raising my four young children. I do believe that you can "have it all" in your career and life. Being a coach aligns with my purpose of helping others accomplish their personal and professional goals with balance.

I did three things to help ease the process when moving from my corporate job to opening my own coaching practice. First, I researched everything related to opening a private practice: for instance, getting a business license, obtaining an office, and getting credentialed as a coach through the International Coaching Federation. Second, I hired a business coach myself to help me move from idea to action. Finally, I trademarked my coaching niche. Getting clarity helps you to choose the right mentors, pursue the right training, and even focus your leisure reading.

As a coach, I help lots of other military moms struggling with work/life balance too, and I remind them that life is intermittently off balance and that is OK and expected. A few tips I recommend are taking classes, hiring a mentor or coach, and keeping a journal.

I love learning and use my daily journal to plan out my next day in detail, as well as reflect on one aspect of my day; recording what I did well and what I would do differently next time. This daily planning and reflection helps me improve a little each day as well as leverage my efforts; for example, if I have an article due for a military spouse publication, I may write about the same topic that I am presenting to a Family Readiness Group meeting. Think about where you can make strides as well as leverage your efforts to work smarter rather than harder.

I also find that planning your next day also keeps you more on target with your goals. By having days planned, it is easier to respond a polite "No thank you" to important requests that don't align with your vision. You can also weave in time for cleaning/organizing and exercising, and your weekly meal plan that is quick and healthy, giving you more energy for those big goals. I also try to schedule lots of guilt-free pleasure time. The laundry and house cleaning will still get done if you schedule in this "fun." I wholeheartedly embrace best-selling author and coach Cheryl Richardson's motto that "There is nothing selfish about self care"!

Krista Wells, Ph.D., Wells Consulting, LLC

The Military Spouse Coach®, *Speaker, Writer, Certified Coach*

www.militaryspousecoach.com

REGISTERED NURSE (RN)

National Average Salary: $30.65 hourly or $63,750 annually

Comments: According to the *Occupational Outlook Handbook*, there are about 2.6 million RNs working in the healthcare field. Job opportunities are expected to be excellent through 2018, although that can vary by location. In a gross generalization of everything they actually do, nurses do the hard and often thankless job of caring for patients.

To work as a RN, you must first graduate from a nursing program. You can do this in one of three ways:

1. Earn a bachelor's degree in nursing (BSN) from a college or university.
2. Earn an associate degree in nursing (ADN) from a community or junior college.
3. Earn a diploma in about three years through a hospital's unique program.

After successfully completing any academic program, you must then also pass the National Council Licensure Examination for Registered Nurses (NCLEX-RN) exam to obtain an RN license. You may need to periodically enroll in coursework to keep your skills and credentials current, as is often the case with any job dependent upon a regulated license or certification.

If you are thinking about becoming a nurse, consider which path you choose to get there. Although all three, along with successfully passing the exam, enable you to be qualified as a nurse, some may not lead you to other jobs down the road. While nursing is a portable job, making it a "smart" one, varying state-licensing requirements could present potential obstacles along the way.

Where They Work:

Registered nurses work in hospitals, stand-alone emergency departments, doctors' offices, hospice settings, K-12 schools, colleges, and universities. They may also be found in corporations or serving as healthcare consultants, and some visit private homes.

Related Jobs:

- Acute Care Nurse
- Critical Care Nurse
- Emergency Medical Technician
- Home Health Aide
- Licensed Practical Nurse
- Licensed Vocational Nurse
- Medical/Dental Assistant
- Nurse Anesthetist
- Nurse Midwife
- Nurse Practitioner
- Nursing Aide, Orderly and Attendant
- Nursing Instructor
- Physical Therapist

For More Information:

- American Association of Colleges of Nursing (AACN) www.aacn.nche.edu
- American Nurses Association (ANA) www.nursingworld.org
- National League for Nursing (NLN) www.nln.org
- American Society of Registered Nurses www.asrn.org
- Also look up specialty nursing associations that focus on your area of expertise. For example, The American College of Nurse Midwives (www.midwife.org).

RELOCATION SPECIALIST

Average National Salary: $34,651 – $68,519

Comments: Not to be confused with real estate agents, relocation specialists are involved in helping families transition their households and, by extension, their lives.

They may help you figure out how to enroll your children in a new school system or connect you with real estate agents who can help you find a new home. They may have local expertise in such areas as real estate, family issues, utilities, banking, taxation, and legal issues.

If you work as a relocation specialist, you might find yourself working for a large corporation that moves its employees around the world or across the U.S. You can find relocation specialists in the military community as well, usually working within the family support centers.

It seems like this would be an ideal smart job for military spouses who have survived more relocations than most. Potential niche customers could include an older population that is downsizing and moving into assisted living facilities as well as military and corporate families.

Where They Work:

Relocation specialists may work in or with a real estate company. Many also maintain a license to sell real estate and combine the services of selling and helping families settle into their new homes. Some work with major corporations that send their employees all over the world. Still others can be found in any sized business within the benefits section of the human resources department. Some specialists also work independently.

Related Jobs:

Real Estate Agent
Corporate Relocation Specialist
Benefits Coordinator

For More Information:

- Worldwide ERC: The Workforce Mobility Association
  www.worldwideerc.org

- Beyond Borders, Inc.
  www.beyondborders.us

A Smart Job Voice of Experience
A PASSION AND A CAREER ALL ON THE SAME CANVAS

As an artist, not only am I following my heart's desire and fulfilling a deep craving within my very soul, I am also able to remain at hand for my family. I set my own hours, deadlines, and goals.

This career travels well, although there are always decisions to make with each move. *Should I pursue local gallery representation? Where should I try to have my work displayed in the community?* I also have to get any local required business licenses. Networking is important and I start reaching out and building connections as soon as I arrive in a new place. The Internet is an integral part of my career and I am careful to keep it up, particularly when we're in the middle of a move.

On the downside, the paychecks aren't regular. When I do sell a painting or two, though, the payoff can be enormous. When we PCS, I have to wait for a majority of my supplies, so sometimes the larger projects have to wait. If I have someone who wants to buy one of my existing paintings, I have to tell them that the work is in transit and I don't know when it will arrive. That is one of the most stressful aspects of this job.

My paintings that are done in wax are extremely fragile and I know that if they are damaged, it is going to be a real battle to be reimbursed for their actual value. I have to make sure the movers pack the paintings properly.

I am a self-taught artist who believes that art is something you either love and want to do, so you put in the hours practicing, or it's not.

My biggest piece of advice to other spouses is to always follow your heart. I know that it's easy to think that you should just take whatever job you can find so that you can help support your family financially, but, honestly, as often as our spouses are gone these days, we really need to take care of our own needs as well as those of our spouse and our children. Follow your dreams. Think of what you really love and then find a way to incorporate that into your daily life and turn that passion into a career.

Mary Christine Farrenkopf-Johnson
Army Spouse and Contemporary Fine Artist
www.facebook.com/pages/Mary-Johnson-Artist/307279116107

TEACHER (K-12)

National Average Salary: $47,100 – $51,180

Comments: Teaching is an honorable smart job choice and, despite various obstacles, many military spouses choose this profession. To work in a public school, you must be licensed, which usually means you have to have a bachelor's degree and have successfully completed an approved teacher education program. These credentials may not be required of teachers who work in private schools. In addition to traditional certification programs offered to help you become a teacher, a number of alternative certification programs are available as well.

Job opportunities are expected to be average, growing at projected rate of 13% through 2018, although that can vary by location. Chances of being hired are greater in inner cities and rural areas as opposed to suburban districts.

Being a teacher and a mobile military spouse seems like a good fit. Anytime, however, a state license or certification process is involved, you need to be aware of the differing requirements and figure out how you're going to deal with them from place to place.

As a mobile teacher, you also face the challenge of trying to establish yourself professionally at a new school every few years. This can be difficult depending upon the existing old school (pun intended) culture. Teachers who are sorting out state certification issues or are waiting to be hired may be able to bide their time by substitute teaching or teaching at a private school.

Where They Work:

Teachers, K-12 and others, as you might guess, work in our public, private, and DoD schools. You can also find them in vocational, college, and university settings as well as in corporate offices. Teachers can also find employment working within companies that specialize in providing educational services such as online tutoring, curriculum development, and textbook creation and editing. They consult with businesses and may also design and develop teaching materials for schools, businesses, and publishing companies.

Related Jobs:

- Childcare Worker
- Coach
- Community College Teacher
- Corporate Trainer
- Counselor
- Librarian
- Post-Secondary Teacher
- Preschool Teacher
- Special Education Teacher
- Substitute Teacher
- Teacher Assistant
- University/College Teacher
- Tutor
- Vocational Teacher

For More Information:

- Department of Defense Education Activity
  www.dodea.edu
- National Center for Alternative Certification
  www.teach-now.org
- Teacher Education Accreditation Council
  www.teac.org
- National Council for Accreditation of Teacher Education
  www.ncate.org
- Association of American Educators
  www.aaeteachers.org

A Smart Job Voice of Experience

TEACHING ALL OVER THE WORLD

Being a teacher fits in with my life as a military spouse. No matter where you go, teachers are always needed. I started my career as a teacher more for the convenience of it, but once I started doing it, I realized how much I really enjoyed it.

Most of the teaching jobs I've had were full time and within the public school systems, removed from the military post. It has been interesting to interact with people who have lives outside of the military. While I enjoy teaching all children, I most prefer working with the younger students because the materials are more integrated and there is more of an opportunity to influence younger people.

Since being stationed overseas, I have also worked with the Department of Defense Education Activity (DoDEA) in Europe, mostly on a substitute-teaching basis. Working as a substitute has provided me with welcomed flexibility. I am able to do the other things that a military lifestyle tends to demand of us, while still working professionally. I also have the increased flexibility to travel more frequently and that's a nice plus when you're stationed in Europe. It has been a good fit for me.

One of the pros about working as a teacher for me, is that you have a natural starting point and an ending one each year. And, even in difficult economic times, good teachers are needed everywhere.

On the negative side, differing state certification requirements can be challenging to meet. You may have your certification to teach, but there always seems to be some little other course or requirement you need on top of what you already have. After a while, the cost of gaining those extras can add up, particularly when you PCS.

If teaching is something you're thinking about, then I would suggest you seek a national board certification. Go for the highest level of certification possible so that when you PCS, you're more likely to already have what you need in terms of the standard. I also suggest you earn your master's degree as soon as possible. The job market is competitive and having that degree, along with a certification, helps.

It also helps if you do your research in advance. If you know the places you could PCS to, find out what is required there before you ever move there. Keep careful track of your completed coursework and carry official (sealed) and unofficial transcripts with you as you move around, to save request and mailing times. Recognize going into the field of teaching as a military spouse that you will need to take care of those things with every move.

Ann Berg
K-12 Teacher and Army Spouse

TRANSLATOR/INTERPRETER

National Average Salary: $28,940 – $52,240

Comments: If you are fluent in a second language, consider being a translator or an interpreter. Job opportunities in our global neighborhood are projected to increase at about 22%, a much faster than average rate. Languages high in demand include Arabic, other Middle Eastern languages, Chinese, Japanese, and Korean. Demand will still be strong for Portuguese, French, Italian, German, and Spanish. Job opportunities for sign language interpreters for the deaf will also be good.

If you have the skill, this is certainly a job that can travel well with you. Finding the corresponding job opportunities may be challenging unless you PCS to a major urban area such as Washington, DC or New York. Depending upon the military community where you are stationed, there may be unique opportunities to work in this field.

This is a smart job choice, particularly for foreign-born military spouses who are fluent in English (as well as their native language) and may have limited federal employment opportunities.

Where They Work:

Translators and interpreters may work in a variety of settings such as within our own military communities and other federal agencies. About 28% currently work in public and private schools, colleges, and universities, and 13% work in healthcare and social assistance. Specific settings include schools, hospitals, courtrooms, businesses, and conference centers. Some translators work within the publishing industry as well.

Related Jobs:

- Adult Literacy Teacher
- K-12 Teacher
- Author
- Writer
- Editor
- Medical Transcriptionist
- Court Reporter
- Tour Guide
- Protocol Specialist
- International Trade Specialist
- Border Patrol Officer
- Intelligence Officer
- Equal Opportunity Specialist
- Corporate Booking Agent

For More Information:
- American Translator Association
  www.atanet.org
- US Department of State, Office of Language Services
  http://languageservices.state.gov
- National Association of Judiciary Interpreters and Translators
  www.najit.org
- International Medical Interpreters Association
  www.imiaweb.org

TRAVEL AGENT

National Average Salary: $23,940 – $38,390

Comments: *A-ruba, Ja-mai-ca...* Now picture in your mind a young and handsome Tom Cruise, easy breezy beach music, and sand between your toes for the proper background effect. You know you want to go there and as a travel agent you might be able to get there less expensively. One of the big perks of coordinating the travel and vacation plans of others is getting to coordinate your own, often at low or no cost.

In the course of a usual day, travel agents assist their clients by advising them about potential destinations and by making transportation and accommodation arrangements. Think back to the last time you tried to do this yourself for an impending PCS move or for a family vacation and you can appreciate their guidance in taming the information overload beast inherent in this job.

Travel agents may work closely with tour operators and other travel agents to put together plans. They may work directly for one or more employers to assist employees with business travel. They use the Internet for scheduling information and making arrangements. They often specialize in knowing about various locations.

Many travel agents receive formal training via programs offered at community colleges, vocational schools, or online. Some agents earn a bachelor's or master's degree in travel and tourism. Skills that will serve you well as a travel agent include: solid computer skills, ability to speak one or more foreign language(s), understanding of world geography and history, and excellent communication and people skills.

Self-employed agents, who make up about 17% of those working in the profession, usually make their earnings from commissions and the service fees they charge their clients. Salaried agents working for travel agents and employers enjoy a steady paycheck and employer-provided benefits.

The job outlook for those in this career is expected to remain steady through 2018, with a possible decline in need as Internet-based searches make the task easier for prospective travelers.

Scam Alert: Beware of "job offers" to be a travel agent that suggest you can make thousands of dollars working from the comfort of your own home. As with any job, if something sounds too good to be true, it probably is. Always get your job information from a reliable and reputable source and not from a multi-level marketing czar wannabe.

Where They Work:

Typically, it's a desk job. You may work from the comfort of your own home in your fuzzy bunny slippers or all dressed up for the general public in a brick-and-mortar travel agency or in a large corporation's travel department.

Related Jobs:

- Tour Guide
- Escorts
- Travel Guide
- Travel Clerk
- Reservation Agent
- Ticket Agent
- Resort Desk Clerk
- Hotel/Motel Clerk
- Concierge

For More Information:

- American Society of Travel Agents
  www.asta.org
- Global Travel
  www.globaltravel.com
- The Travel Institute
  www.thetravelinstitute.com
- National Association of Career Travel Agents
  www.nacta.com

- Professional Association of Travel Hosts (PATH)
  www.path4hosts.com
- National Business Travel Association (GBTA)
  www.gbta.org/Pages/default.aspx
- Outside Sales Support Network
  www.ossn.com

WRITER

National Average Salary: $38,150 – $75,060

Comments: If you want a job that travels easily with you, call yourself a writer. Many people do, whether they can actually write well or not.

Employment outlook is expected to grow about as fast as average – from 7 to 13%.

Writing jobs can be found across all industries and in many different forms. Many writers work in salaried positions while others work on a freelance or contract basis. About 70% of all writers are self-employed.

If technology is your strength in addition to writing, then you offer potential employers a double win.

Writers often specialize in areas such as fiction, nonfiction, technical writing, ghostwriting, grant writing, copy writing, or blogging.

Where They Work:

Writers can be found behind keyboards everywhere. They work in offices or from home. You can find them in newsrooms, at public relation firms, at colleges and universities, and in virtually any business or non-business setting.

Related Jobs:

• Technical writer	• Copy writer	• Grant writer
• News Analyst	• Author	• Public relations
• Reporter	• Novelist	• Advertiser
• Correspondent	• Poet	• Publisher
• Announcer	• Blogger	• Editor

For More Information:

- American Society of Journalists and Authors
  www.asja.org
- The Association of Writers and Writing Programs,
  George Mason University
  www.awpwriter.org
- Association of Writers & Writing
  www.awpwriter.org
- American Business Media
  www.americanbusinessmedia.com
- National Writers Union
  www.nwu.org

A Smart Job Voice of Experience

BLOGGING ABOUT THE MEAT AND POTATOES OF LIFE

The true benefit to being a military spouse blogger is the completely free outlet for creative expression. Blogging can be done anywhere, anytime, be it from an iPhone in Japan or a desktop computer in New Jersey. No office, babysitters, or resumes required – all one needs is an Internet connection and a few minutes to set up a free blog on Wordpress, Blogspot, or other free blog template sites.

My weekly blog column, "The Meat and Potatoes of Life," has given me a real sense of achievement, sometimes difficult for military spouses to find, and has opened doors to other writing opportunities.

The disadvantage of this particular "job" is that blogs alone make absolutely no money unless they offer advertising, affiliate marketing, paid subscriptions, or some product/service for sale. In order to add these money-making extras, one must first establish a blog that attracts a high number of viewers each week, using social media sites, e-mailing, and other forms of publicity.

Any military spouse who is a good writer can succeed at blogging as long as she/he is willing to put in the time each week to write and market their site. Whether the blog itself makes money or not, it can be an incredible source of pride and fulfillment, which could lead to paid freelance work, speaking engagements, and even book deals!

Lisa Smith Molinari,
Navy Spouse, Columnist and Blogger
www.themeatandpotatoesoflife.com

A Short List of Other Smart Job Choices to Consider:

- Actuary
- Call center representative
- Career counselor
- Childcare provider
- Community volunteer
- Computer programmer
- Computer systems analyst
- Curriculum developer
- Dental hygienist
- Ebay guru
- Event planner
- Fundraiser
- Home stager
- Image consultant
- Information technology specialist
- Jewelry designer
- Landscape designer
- Massage therapist
- Online researcher
- Online tutor
- Photographer
- Salesperson
- Social media strategist
- Software engineer
- Statistician
- Travel writer
- Virtual assistant
- Web designer/developer

PART II
Smart Job Search Strategies

4

Finding a Job Wherever You Are Stationed

EVERYONE KNOWS THAT the best place to be stationed is the one you just left behind or the one that waits for you. Seldom do we find complete satisfaction in what is ironically called "the present." That may be a good thing or not, but it's an accepted reality of military life in many instances.

Another accepted and oft-lamented reality is that some duty stations have better employment options than others.

Let's be honest. What highly marketable and professionally motivated spouse wouldn't, on at least some level, want to be stationed in Northern Virginia even with its infamous traffic congestion?

One-horse towns where we often end up stationed may provide new degrees of appreciable quaintness, but no amount of unbridled optimism will produce jobs out of thin air.

It would be easy to complain about those types of places and the difficulty in getting hired there – or anywhere these days for that matter. But complaining, however cathartic the process, only wastes valuable time and energy that could be channeled in more productive ways.

Besides, the reality du jour is that times are tough for everyone. In a truly perverse way that almost makes you want to cry, we military spouses are somehow better equipped on one level to handle difficult economic times. We're used to having it tough, right?

More often than not, we choose to pack up our households and move to whatever far end of the globe our servicemembers are sent to serve. When we do, we usually experience one of these six employment outcomes in our ID-card carrying travels:

1. You find the job of your dreams.
2. You accept a job 360° from the one you set out to get.
3. You work in a "fringe" job somewhere along the edges of your ideal one.
4. You go into business for yourself.
5. You volunteer.
6. You don't work at all.

If ever there was a case for having a smart job that can travel with you, this is it.

Setting Yourself Up for Job Search Success

To get a job, you have to know how to find one. It doesn't get any simpler.

On the plus side, many job search skills are transferable and you will use them more than once in your lifetime, as a military spouse. As a bonus, you can share what you know or learn with your uniformed spouse when the time comes for his or her transition or retirement from service.

Even if you think you already know how to find a job, review the basics provided in this chapter. You don't look for a job every day. If you don't keep certain skills honed, they dull over time. Additionally, new social media job search strategies have evolved, and you need to use them to your advantage.

To set the stage for job search success, you need to:

- Understand the current conditions of the local job market you're targeting
- Know whom you can turn to for employment assistance
- Organize your job search activities for greater effectiveness
- Enhance your online career identity for increased visibility

Understand the Current Conditions of the Local Job Market You're Targeting

Location matters. To develop realistic job search expectations, you need a basic understanding of an area's employment dynamics. If the local chamber of commerce, for example, has just persuaded a major corporation to relocate their headquarters to the town, you want to know about it because they could possibly be your next employer.

While you don't have to be an economist, it would help to find answers to these seven key questions:

1. What are the biggest industries found in the community? Is everything centered on or around the military installation, or could the town survive on its own without the presence of the defense industry? Is there a major medical center nearby or a big university? Is manufacturing dominant or is tourism the big community rainmaker?

2. What types of jobs are found locally within those industries?

3. How much do employees earn on the average? Which industry pays the best? The worst?

4. Who are the specific employers and what industries do they fall under?

5. What is the fastest growing local industry? Name the one that is showing signs of declining employment. In other words, who is hiring and who isn't?

6. How are jobs filled? Do employers recruit and hire directly for positions within their companies? Are employment agencies used to provide staffing services? Does the local Department of Labor play a strong role?

7. What is the local unemployment rate? How does it compare to the national one?

These resources, and ones like them, can give you the answers:

- Career OneStop, America's Service Locator, State Profiles
  http://www.servicelocator.org/StateProfiles.asp

- The state or city government home page
- The local chamber of commerce home page
- Local news sources, print and online
- The employment readiness center on the military installation
- Directory of Military Installations (see Local Community Information) http://www.militaryinstallations.dod.mil/pls/psgprod/f?p=MI:EN-TRY:0

Know Whom to Turn to for Employment Assistance

As a military spouse, you have a team of experts available to assist you in your job search. Why not use them?

The Employment Readiness Program

Located at the military family service/support center nearest you is an employment readiness program. Use it. It doesn't matter if you are an Air Force spouse and the nearest base is an Army post. You can use them regardless. It doesn't cost you a dime.

The employment readiness program:

- Provides you with job search training in a group or on a one-on-one basis.
- Helps you to identify and enhance your marketable skills.
- Assists you with preparing your resumes and cover letters.
- Helps you to prepare for the interview process, from beginning to end.
- Provides you with free Internet access.
- Offers you access to a resource library.
- Shows you what jobs are available locally, nationally, and internationally.

Military OneSource Spouse Career Center (SCC)

Military OneSource's SCC is an invaluable online career center that comes with the added bonus of access to experienced career counselors over the telephone. Counselors can help you perfect your resume and your interviewing skills. They can help you figure out a plan of action for going to college. They can help you explore different career options and connect you to others who can help you even more. To use these services call 1-800-342-9647, or visit https://www.militaryonesource.com/MOS/FindInformation/Category/MilitarySpouseCareerAdvancementAccounts.aspx.

> **Hot Tip:** You can also subscribe to a *Spouse Employment and Education Newsletter*, full of fabulous information and advice, and it will be emailed to you monthly at no cost.

The Military Spouse Employment Partnership (MSEP)

Go to www.msepjobs.militaryonesource.mil and you can take advantage of the newly launched DoD Military Spouse Employment Partnership Job Board. Designed to expand career opportunities for spouses worldwide, the site allows you to:

- Obtain resume writing and job search assistance
- Search for national and international jobs
- Link up to MSEP partners who are receptive to hiring military spouses

Again, there is no cost to you. It's a good thing. Register. Search. Get hired. What's not to like in this process?

The Local Department of Labor

The local Department of Labor is intimately connected with the employers it services. You need a job. They know about jobs. You can apply for those jobs through them. You may be able to attend job search assistance workshops as well.

Other reasons to access their brand of expertise:

- You might be eligible for unemployment benefits and if you are, you apply for those benefits through the local Department of Labor. Be sure you check with the state where you are stationed and working *before* resigning your job or leaving on a PCS move to inquire about potential benefits.
- You can research local area employment dynamics through them.

To find out where the nearest State Department of Labor is located, visit http://www.dol.gov/dol/location.htm.

Local Job Search Support Groups

Job search support groups come in all shapes and sizes. Some of them are free of charge and some charge a fee for attendance. If you decide to visit one, you may benefit in these ways:

- You can take advantage of the power of 10. You meet 10 other people who are also looking for a job and you can all share job leads with each other. It's called networking and it is the best way to get a job.
- Expert advice is often available from others attending and from key speakers who may be invited to address the group.
- A job search can be difficult and lonely. Meeting others who are in the same situation can be helpful as you share experiences and offer morale support to one another.

To find a local job search support group, check with the employment readiness program manager on the installation nearest you. Someone from the Department of Labor, Chamber of Commerce, or local college career center might also know of area groups. Online, look at www.job-hunt.org for an unofficial but thorough listing of job search support groups by most states. You can also contact Military OneSource for assistance at 1-800-342-9647.

Your Family Readiness Group

If you are new to a community and need to know where to go, consider tapping into the expertise of those in your unit's military family readiness group (FRG). By definition, the FRG is more than just a place to eat cupcakes, meet new people, and let your kids get to know each other. FRGs are an excellent resource for information, providing self-help and referral in times of deployment and otherwise. Someone there may know the answers to the questions you have or may be able to point you in a good direction. And, after you know everything, you can give back to some other spouse by being the expert. Everybody wins, don't you think?

The Transition Assistance Program (TAP)

If you meet the eligibility requirements, use the services of the DoD's TAP (http://www.turbotap.org), designed to smooth the transition of military servicemembers and their families leaving active duty. Working with the DoD, the DoL, and Veterans Administration (VA), TAP offers eligible users:

- DoD preseparation counseling
- DoL-sponsored employment workshops
- VA benefits briefing
- Disabled TAP (DTAP)
- Career counseling

If you are stationed in an Army community, TAP is known as the Army Career and Alumni Program (ACAP). Same program. Different name only.

Organize Your Job Search Activities for Greater Effectiveness

It's one thing to say you want to find a good job. It's quite another to actually go out there and do it. The hard work of finding a job will come easier if you organize your efforts first.

Here are some tips to help you do that:

1. **Make the business of finding your next employer a job in and of itself.** Dedicate a set number of hours consistently each day to the process.

2. **Set up an office to conduct your job search.** Your office may be the kitchen table and a laptop. It may be a quiet corner at the public library or local coffee shop where grande mocha java inspires your energy levels. Wherever it is, it is the place where you focus 100% of your attention on finding your next job.

3. **Set and obtain daily and weekly goals.** Goals are an important part of your job search efforts. Certainly, the ultimate goal is to get hired in a job that you want. In order to reach that ultimate goal, however, you have to do a lot of other tasks in between.

Those tasks can become the basis for your daily and weekly goals that will eventually lead to the accomplishment of landing a job.

For example, your weekly goal might be to research five employers and apply for five jobs. A corresponding daily goal might be to focus on researching and applying for a job with one employer each day.

Having specific daily and weekly goals will consistently move you closer to reaching your overall goal of employment.

4. **Manage the paperwork effectively.** Vacancy announcements, resumes, cover letters, and copies of job application forms that aren't organized in appropriate folders, electronically or otherwise, can create one big and overwhelming mess.

   Develop your own method of taming the paperwork madness and manage it daily. A mere five minutes of filing can save you hours over the long haul when you need to find one specific document. Be sure to clearly identify stacks or folders so you can easily find what you need when you need it.

5. **Keep track of your individual job search activities.** You can use a plain spiral notebook, a leather-bound journal, a spreadsheet, or the notes application on your cell phone or e-reader. It doesn't matter how you do it; it is just important that you do it in the first place.

   The kind of information you will want to record in some form is:

   - Date you made contact with a company or a person
   - Name of business you made contact with (include address/ web address)
   - How the contact was made (in person, online chat, telephone, email)
   - Name and contact information for person you spoke with
   - Type of contact (job application, resume, inquiry, interview, or other)
   - Action (what came out of it)
   - Next step date (when/if you will follow up)
   - Next step action (how are you going to follow up?)

6. **Keep yourself focused and organized.** Don't let those initial organization efforts be for nothing. Keep them up. Review your progress or lack thereof on a daily basis. Focus on achieving those daily and weekly goals you set. Become a master note-taker and conqueror of the infamous To-Do List.

Enhance Your Online Career Identity for Increased Visibility

Potential employers may already have made that first impression of you before you have even met them. You can thank the Internet for that.

Before you launch your job search, you may want to consider shoring up your online professional identity first.

- **Search for yourself.** Using your name and variations of it, search web, video, and image results from Google, Yahoo, and AOL.

- **Alert yourself.** You want to know what the online chatter is about you. You can find out easily enough by setting up an online alert that notifies you via email that your name has been mentioned somewhere. Start with www.google.com/alert.

- **Review and adjust privacy settings on social sites you frequent.** Be stingy about whom you let into your inner online world.

- **Pay someone to do it for you.** If you find yourself at a total loss for taming your cyber skeletons, you can always pay someone else to do it for you. Companies like Brand-Yourself (www.brand-yourself.com) will bury any bad Google results and help you to create a strong online brand.

After you've cleaned your cyber-closet, consider adding some new features to it that will increase future search engine results positively.

- **Start a professionally based blog.** You know stuff. Strut it on a blog that others, including potential employers, can easily read. A well-written and maintained blog is like a bonus to your resume. It gives others more insight to your communication skills and to your level of involvement in your professional passions.

Starting one is relatively easy:

- Analyze other blogs first and then plan your own.

- Decide on a topic in line with your area of professional expertise.

- Create a catchy yet professional name for your blog.

- Buy a domain name in the same name as your blog.

- Publish your written entries. You can either pay someone to do it or you can host it for free at some sites such as WordPress.

- Keep your blog current. You don't have to post an entry every day but do it consistently so that any readers or employers who end up following it won't be disappointed.

- Learn about the importance of keywords for search engine optimization.

• **Establish a website.** Thankfully, you don't need to be a computer scientist who understands the inner workings of HTML coding to create an attractive web presence. You need to be able to point, click, and sometimes pay.

There are a number of online website building services that can help you easily create a webpage such as Go Daddy.com, Google, Yahoo, Devhub, SnapPages, Intuit, and Wix, just to name a few. Some offer free services while others may charge you after a trial period.

The hard part in the process is figuring out exactly what you want to go on your site before you actually create it.

Tracking Down Job Opportunities

There are many ways to track down job openings, with some ways working faster than others.

• You can apply for a job that is being advertised and actively recruited.
• You can submit your resume for consideration whether there is a job opening or not.
• You can ask an employer to create a position for you.
• You can volunteer somewhere while trying to get hired in a paying job there.

- You can start your own business.
- You can take a job that is currently available and discreetly continue looking for a better one in your spare time.

There are also different ways you can work, beyond the traditional 9-5 job:

- You can share a job with someone else.
- You can work flextime, varying your start and finish times.
- You can work part-time.
- You can work on a compressed schedule, such as 10 hours a day Monday through Thursday, with Fridays off.
- You can work on a rotating schedule.
- You can telecommute.
- You can work on a project/assignment basis.

Try to think outside the usual construct of what a job has to be, and embrace all the possibilities that it can be and how you can do it.

The Importance of Networking

Job opportunities can be found anywhere. Most of them, as you probably know all too well, are filled by word of mouth. Someone connects someone else to a job or to some other person who knows of one. It's called **networking** and it is the number one way, hands down, to find a job.

If you want to find a good job anywhere, you have to be able to network for it.

You have to be able to tell others that you are in the market for a new job. You have to be able to explain the short version of your professional background and what you hope to do in the future.

It works to your advantage if you can come across as an engaging, authentic, and interesting person.

You can network with anyone, anywhere. You can expand your network by meeting more people, building stronger bonds with the ones you already know, and by becoming more involved in your community.

To make your network a good one, don't just expect it to work for you. You need to return the favor and help others out along the way.

Sources of Job Opportunities

Whether you like it or not, networking is the best way to land a job. There is no getting around it. You **have** to get out and network with others. When you think about brick-and-mortar or virtual places to go to network or to find out about jobs directly, you'll want to consider the ones listed below. On or off the installation, these organizations or types of businesses, not listed in any special order, could lead you to your next job.

- **Federal appropriated and non-appropriated fund job opportunities** on the installation. See Chapter 5 for more information on how to specifically locate and apply for federal jobs at www.usajobs.gov.

- **The local Department of Labor** provides information about state and local city jobs. You can also access state job banks, private sector job sites, government-sponsored job sites and recruiting and staffing services directly from the DoL's CareerOneStop website (www.careeronestop.org).

- **The Military Spouse Employment Partnership** (www.msepjobs. militaryonesource.mil) is a new job board for military spouses and a must-click site. You can learn more about MSEP, under *"Know Who to Turn to for Employment Assistance,"* earlier in this chapter, on page 56.

- **The Military OneSource Spouse Career Center** counselors help you to get the right job in the right career by working with MSEP, USAJobs, and CareerOneStop.

- **Military associations** frequently offer spouses who are members resume critiques, workshops, and career counseling. They may host major job fairs such as the ones sponsored by the Military Officers Association of America (www.moaa.org), or they may create networking opportunities like the National Military Spouse Network (www. nationalmilitaryspousenetwork.org) does. Others, such as the Association of the United States Army (www.ausa.org), keep members updated on spouse employment initiatives, education, and scholarship opportunities. There are many different associations. Some of them cater to all branches of the service family, while others focus primarily on one branch. Take advantage of the good things they offer.

- **The Military Spouse Corporate Career Network** (www.msccn.org) has recently teamed with Kenexa Inc and DirectEmployers to create the largest military spouse dedicated job bank in the world.

- **Professional networking sites,** such as LinkedIn, and social ones, such as Facebook.

- Through informal virtual contacts made through **online communities** hosted by sites such as Military OneSource, CinC-House, Army Wife Network, Milspouse.com, MilitarySOS, and Military. com. There's always something you can learn from someone who has been stationed where you are now.

- **Defense contractors** that provide products or services to the DoD. The` top 25 technology-focused biggies in 2011, according to Washington Technology, the online authority for government contractors and partners, are as follows:

  1. Lockheed Martin Corporation
  2. Northrop Grumman Corporation
  3. Boeing Company
  4. Raytheon Company
  5. General Dynamics Corporation
  6. Science Applications International Corporation (SAIC)
  7. Hewlett-Packard Company
  8. L-3 Communications Corporation
  9. Booz Allen Hamilton
  10. KBR, Inc.
  11. Computer Sciences Corporation
  12. DynCorp International, Inc.
  13. Harris Corporation
  14. CACI International Incorporated
  15. Dell Computer Corporation
  16. ITT Corporation
  17. BAE Systems, Inc.
  18. Verizon Communications, Inc.
  19. Fluor Corporation
  20. Jacobs Engineering Group, Inc.
  21. IBM Corporation

22. ManTech International Corporation
23. United Technologies Corporation
24. Battelle Memorial Institute
25. Deloitte

Other companies and organizations also provide services and products to the DoD. The next time you are on a military installation, note the cross-section of industries and businesses that you see providing services to the military community, such as banking/finance, education, food service, and retail.

- **Nonprofit** doesn't mean non-paying, and there are plenty of good jobs available with organizations such as the Red Cross, the United Services Organization (USO), and the Fisher House Foundation. For an extensive database of nonprofit organizations, visit Idealist. org (www.idealist.org) or Guidestar (www2.guidestar.org).

- **Department of Defense Education Activity** (www.dodea.edu) employs about 12,000 people worldwide as it serves the children of military servicemembers and DoD civilian employees. It operates 192 public schools in 14 districts located in 12 foreign countries, seven states, Guam, and Puerto Rico. You can find out about openings at USA Jobs (www.usajobs.gov).

- **Defense Commissary Agency (DeCA)** (www.commissaries.com), your on-installation grocery-shopping venue, may also be a source of employment. They currently employ more than 18,000 people throughout 14 countries. Job opportunities are often available across several departments including customer service, receiving, produce, meat, management support, and grocery, with career progression being a possibility. You can apply for positions through USA Jobs (www.usajobs.gov).

- X marks the spot – or so **Air Force/Army Exchange** (formerly AAFES) hopes. The Exchange, along with **Navy Exchange** (NEX), offers spouses competitive salaries, a 401(k) plan, and a defined pension plan. Jobs often exist in areas such as sales, human resources, logistics, finance and accounting, equal opportunity, information technology, and marketing, among others.

- **No-fee temporary agencies** are often well connected to local employers and know what positions need to be filled. Employers will often hire an employee through a temporary agency first before hiring them full-time directly. No-fee is the operative word here. Don't pay for someone else to find you a job. Some big agencies that can be found throughout the U.S. are Adecco, Manpower, Kelly Services, Olsten, Interim Services, Aquent, Robert Half International, Westaff, OfficeTeam, and AppleOne.

- **Employment search professionals,** other than no-fee temporary agencies, that do not charge you for placement. Some search firms may recruit en masse for specific industries such as healthcare or finance on either a contingency or retained basis. Headhunters or recruiters may work more closely with you to match your skills to potential employers.

- **The careers, jobs or employment links posted on individual company websites.**

- **Job fairs**, virtual and otherwise, usually provide you with ample employment leads. You can learn about upcoming job fairs, on and off the installation, through the family center's employment readiness program.

- **Professional associations** often provide links to employment opportunities for their members. If you are a member and you are networking, you get access to leads that are often closed to the general public.

- **Major online job boards**, such as Monster.com, CareerBuilder.com, and Simplyhired.com.

- **Newspaper** classified advertisements and news articles highlighting local business updates, print and online.

- **Inside yourself.** It could be that you are a successful business just waiting for the right moment in time to finally realize it. See the Go-To Resources on page 157 for links to small business sites that that can help you realize this dream.

More Smart Choice Job Search Strategies

- **Accept the reality that a true job search never ends.** You should be forever looking to the next step in your professional life.

- **Embrace the importance of lifelong learning.** You may have earned a college degree, but you don't know everything. Yet.

- **If at all possible, start your job search at a new duty station long before you even get there.** You can always do the cumbersome employer and local area research in advance. You can start to reach out and connect with those in the community before your arrival.

- **Be sure to line up your references while you still have access to them.** As you ask people to be your reference, coach them about what you would prefer they highlight about you to potential employers who may call them in the future.

- **Ask for written letters of recommendation before you leave a job.** You may never use them but you want to have them just in case.

- **Keep your references in your active network.** Don't ask someone you respect to be your reference and then lose touch with them.

- **Keep updated on new job search practices.** Things change. Who would have thought 10 or 15 years ago that social media would have the impact it does today?

- **Try to keep your professional life separate from your personal one online,** even though it will be difficult if not ultimately impossible. Perhaps the key is to balance the two as best as you can to minimize the damage when your online worlds collide. Because they will eventually collide. Don't post anything about yourself that could reflect negatively on you and turn a prospective employer off.

- **If you have the flexibility, consider volunteering part-time while you are searching for a new job.** It will keep your skills current and keep you in an information loop that doesn't always exist when you're sitting at home.

- **Through whatever means, keep your job skills current.** Read technical or professional trade journals. Take classes online or in person. Keep certificates or licenses up to date and look to future requirements well in advance of PCS moves.

- **Keep in contact with mobile friends.** As a military spouse, you probably know people all over the world. You know them from places you have been stationed, clubs you've been a part of or youth sport sidelines you've shared with other parents. If you have to wonder whom you can network with, then you're just not thinking hard enough about the big picture as it relates to your personal address book.

- **Develop a short sales pitch or elevator speech about yourself** to use when the opportunity presents itself. See *Tips for Creating a 60-Second Pitch* below.

- **If you don't have a mentor, get one or two of them.** A mentor is someone who can share his or her wisdom with you, someone who has a level of expertise or connectivity that you can learn from.

TIPS FOR CREATING A 60-SECOND PITCH

Networking opportunities can happen anywhere and at any time. You want to be prepared should you have the chance to put in a good word for yourself. A 60-second pitch, also known as a one-minute pitch or networking sales byte, is an excellent tool that you can use to put in a good word or two about yourself.

In essence, it briefly answers the question "What can you tell me about yourself?"

A 60-second pitch can be used in moments that accommodate only a few words, or it can be expanded into a longer pitch if the situation calls for it. Regardless of how long your pitch turns out to be, it will be most effective if it is uniquely targeted to a specific situation or job opportunity.

Keep these tips in mind when creating your 60-second pitch:

- Make every sentence count and, remember, shorter is better.
- Strive to create interest in yourself as a potential job candidate.
- Emphasize results that you have accomplished that could apply in the present situation.
- Keep your pitch focused on what you can do for the employer, and not what they can do for you.
- Don't memorize your 60-second pitch. It will sound too rehearsed.
- Speak conversationally and maintain good eye contact.

Remember, employers are usually focused on the bottom line. They want to know how you can make the company money while reducing costs and saving time in the process.

- **Embrace LinkedIn and similar sites used for professional networking purposes.** Update your profile. Join one or two professional groups and contribute your thoughts.

- **Use Twitter, as well, in your job search.** Make sure your profile reflects a professional presence. Use the background space to sell yourself. Include links to your resume, your blog, and/or your website. Tweet about your job search efforts but do so in an **employer-friendly** manner, without criticizing anyone.

- **Observe proper email etiquette.** Etiquette tips for communicating by email with employers during a job search include:

  - Avoid using funky or family email addresses such as coolchick1@yahoo.com, BillSueLeslieJohn@gmail.com, or TheJohnsonFamily@verizon.net.

  - Don't use attention-getting and cheesy looking email addresses like HRJobSeeker57@gmail.com or HireMeJBK@yahoo.com.

  - Check your email messages daily while you are in the process of looking for a job. Be sure you check the email address that you have posted on your resumes as your point of contact.

  - When communicating with a potential employer, use appropriate business language, avoiding acronyms, slang, unfinished thoughts and sentences, and incorrect grammar or punctuation marks.

- **Follow proper telephone etiquette.** Telephone etiquette tips to use during a job search include:

  - Note the correct area code, telephone number, and time zone if the employer will need to know that information in order to contact you from a different location.

  - If possible, use a landline telephone with a clear connection for talking to employers rather than a cell phone that may have a tendency to break up periodically.

  - If you have a music recording on your cell phone for someone to listen to the music until the person answers, drop it during the time you are looking for a position. You may like it, but others may find it annoying.

- Act interested when you get a phone call, and use inflection in your voice to convey your enthusiasm. You don't have the benefit of body language over the phone, so you have to "show" your interest through your voice.

- **When your job search effort seems stalled, try to figure out why.** Don't just keep doing the same thing and expect different results. Einstein said that, right? He seems like he might have known what he was talking about.

  - Get someone else to review your resume. Maybe he or she can detect something that you haven't noticed…like something that just doesn't work. Accept any constructive criticism and address it if it applies.

  - Pick up the telephone and call the last couple of employers you interviewed who didn't hire you, and try to get the real reasons why.

  - Change direction. You may not have to completely abandon one professional track for another, just move your sights a shade to the right or left and see if other opportunities might jump out at you as a result.

  - Re-ignite your network and see if you can't develop any outside traction on your search efforts.

- **Follow through with every single lead.** It may not lead to the kind of job you have in mind, but it could lead to a possibility for a different one.

- **Keep your emotions in check** and don't take rejection personally.

- **Help other military spouses to find good jobs along the way, too.** What goes around will eventually come around to you, and you deserve the best.

- **Lower your stress.** The business of finding a job is stressful. It can be frustrating and cause you to ingest great amounts of totally unnecessary calories. Guard against such extremism by taking care of yourself physically, mentally, and spiritually.

SELF-EMPLOYMENT:
ARE YOU READY TO BE YOUR OWN BOSS?

According to the Small Business Administration, over 99% of employer firms are classified as small businesses and they employ over half of all private sector employees. It has been proven that small businesses create jobs, having generated 64% of net new jobs over the past 15 years. A whopping 52% of such ventures are home-based. Perhaps you should consider creating your own job by becoming self-employed.

Y   N

❏ ❏ Are you a self-starter?

❏ ❏ Are you prepared to work long hours with no pay?

❏ ❏ Do you have a skill, service, or access to a product that others will buy?

❏ ❏ Do you know what makes it different than others already out there like it?

❏ ❏ Do you know how are you going to market it to others?

❏ ❏ Are you a decision-maker?

❏ ❏ Do you have a solid business plan?

❏ ❏ Do you know which legal structure is best suited for your business?

❏ ❏ Do you know where you would run your business from?

❏ ❏ If military housing, can you get approval for working out of there?

❏ ❏ Do you need to earn a steady paycheck?

❏ ❏ Do you have the necessary start-up capital, if applicable?

❏ ❏ Do you have the real support of your uniformed spouse?

❏ ❏ Do you have the necessary equipment/supplies to run your business?

❏ ❏ Do you have basic accounting and management skills?

❏ ❏ Are you aware of local/state/federal licensing and taxation requirements?

❏ ❏ Could this business PCS with you easily?

If you answered more Yes than No above, then self-employment might be a potential direction for you to explore.

Even if you answered No more but you have a burning desire to learn what you need to in order to come up with more Yes answers, self-employment might still be a viable option for you after doing the research.

For links to valuable small business resources online, see the "Self-Employment Assistance" section located in the Go-To Resources section on page 171.

5

Federally Speaking...

DESPITE THE FRUSTRATING bureaucratic and lengthy hiring experiences many spouses report having to go through in order to obtain a position with the federal government, for better or worse, it remains a smart job choice in the bigger employment picture.

Working for the Government

There are definite advantages in federal employment. Here are a few that make this option enticing.

- Federal jobs often exist wherever you get stationed, making the case for potential employment continuity.

- Federal jobs pay fairly well compared to private industry. When there isn't a freeze in place, employees can expect annual pay and in-step increases.

- It's hard to get fired from a federal job. You have to screw up in a big way, and as a result, there is an illusion of job security. But in the current poor economy, nothing is certain.

- If the opportunities exist, you can get promoted.

- The insurance benefits are fabulous, with options to enroll in health, life, long-term care, dental, and vision plans. Flexible spending accounts (FSAs) are also available to help you offset those uncovered and out-of-pocket expenses.

- There are retirement benefits as well as paid holidays, vacation time, and sick days.

- Federal employees often have access to exceptional training and development opportunities.

Of course, there are disadvantages as well.

- The U.S. government will be slashing dollars wherever it can to rein in the monumental debt our nation carries. Some savings will result from reducing the federal workforce; that could affect you, someone you know, or a position billet you had hoped to be hired into.

- The recruitment and hiring processes are often long, drawn out, challenging, confusing, and even conflicting from one duty station to the other.

- People who have federal jobs don't want to leave them, making it harder for someone on the outside to get hired. On one level, it's understandable. Anyone who has a good job these days should try to keep it. On the other hand, if you are someone who PCS's in and out of communities, your skill level options may become limited as a result, making it more difficult to land a job.

- Advancement can be an issue too. Let's assume you accept a lower level GS job to get in the federal door. Career advancement will be slow. It doesn't always matter that you are educationally qualified and have a good work history; you're stuck trying to climb a painfully time-consuming ladder.

- If you happen to be one of the many foreign-born military spouses without U.S. citizenship, you will not be eligible to work in civil service positions, regardless of professional credentials obtained elsewhere.

Hiring Authorities and Preferences

To minimize the disruptions often found in military families due to multiple PCS moves, servicemember disabilities and deaths, specific hiring authorities and preferences have been established to help you get a job within the federal government.

You may already know they exist and that they are supposed to be helpful, but you just don't completely understand how.

Let's just say that you wouldn't be the first person to read over the guidance provided and then wonder what it all meant.

It may help you to get through it, if you understand this simple statement from the outset:

> *Any appointment authority or hiring preference doesn't automatically guarantee you a job just because you are a military spouse.*

You still need to bring qualifications to the table in order to be considered for a job. That seems fair, don't you think?

Below are summaries, adapted from the published official guidance given on www.fedshirevets.gov, the U.S. Office of Personnel Management's government-wide veterans employment website:

1. Military Spouse Appointing Authority

This authority allows agencies to appoint a military spouse without competition. Agencies can choose to use this authority when filling competitive service positions on a temporary (not to exceed one year), term (between one and four years), or permanent basis.

Worth noting here is that an **authority** is not a **hiring preference**. An appointing authority only provides for non-competitive entry into the competitive service. Spouses do not have a selection priority over other qualified applicants under this authority. Agencies don't have to use it if they don't want to, and this authority doesn't take precedence over other appointment tools.

You can use this authority if your active duty spouse receives a PCS move, has a 100% disability rating, or has died while on active duty. Each of these categories has different eligibility criteria:

- **To use the authority as a result of a PCS move:** You have to be on the orders and actually relocate to the new duty station. Military spouses can only be appointed within the reasonable daily commuting distance of the new duty station. If you are going to use this authority, then you must do so within two years of the PCS move. You will need to provide a copy of your servicemember's PCS orders.

- **To use the authority based on a 100% disability rating:** You are eligible if your active duty spouse retired under Chapter 61 of Title 10, U.S. Code with a 100% disability rating from the military. Eligibility is also extended if the active duty servicemember retired or was released from active duty and has a 100% disability rating from the VA or his or her branch of service. There is no geographic limitation on this one, but you will, of course, be required to provide documentation supporting your spouse's disability.

- **To use the authority based on a servicemember's death:** If your servicemember spouse was killed while on active duty and you have not remarried, you are eligible to use the authority based on his or her death. There are no geographic limitations, but you will need to provide supporting documentation of the death and your marital status at the time of death.

2. Military Spouse Preference (MSP)

Military Spouse Preference (MSP) is a Department of Defense (DoD) specific preference that stems from Public Law 99-145 and is applicable to positions being filled only within the DoD in the United States, its territories and possessions, and in overseas areas.

It is not the same thing as the Military Spouse Appointing Authority described above.

It applies to military spouses only within the commuting area of the permanent duty station of the sponsor.

It only applies if you married the military sponsor before the reporting date to the sponsor's new duty assignment.

If your military servicemember is separating or retiring from the military, you cannot use MSP.

Spouse preference eligibility begins 30 days prior to the sponsor's reporting date to the new duty station and continues through the tour until the spouse accepts or declines a continuing (permanent) appropriated or non-appropriated fund position from any federal agency within the commuting area.

If you are PCS'ing overseas, you cannot receive preference until you arrive at the overseas location.

There is no time limit to the number of times a spouse preference may be exercised when applying for non-continuing positions – positions that are temporary, time limited, or not on a fixed work schedule.

You can be simultaneously referred for permanent and temporary positions until you accept or decline a continuing position. If you are placed in a non-continuing position, MSP eligibility for other non-continuing positions will be suspended until 60 days prior to the expiration of the non-continuing position.

To learn more sordid details about the MSP, you can access the DoD Instruction 1404.12: Employment of Spouses of Active Duty Members Stationed Worldwide (January 12, 1989) at DoD Issuances (http://www.dtic. mil/whs/directives/).

You can also pay a visit to the family support center on the military installation nearest you and ask the Employment Readiness manager about it.

3. Family Member Preference (Derived Preference)

Derived Preference is where you, as a military spouse, a widow or widower, or even the mother of a veteran, may be eligible to claim veterans' preference when your veteran is unable to use it. If you are eligible to use this derived preference, then you are given something called an XP Preference (10 points) in appointment if you meet the eligibility criteria.

Military spouses are eligible when their veteran has a service-connected disability and has been unable to qualify for any position within the civil service.

Do not confuse this preference with the Military Spouse Preference found only in the DoD and described above. They are two different hiring mechanisms.

If you are a widow or a widower, then you are eligible to use the derived preference if:

- You and your spouse were married at the time of death.
- You have not remarried, or your remarriage was annulled.
- Your veteran served during a war or during the period April 28, 1952 through July 1, 1955, or in a campaign or expedition for which a campaign medal has been authorized.
- **Or** your servicemember spouse died while on active duty during a war or during the period April 28, 1952 through July 1, 1955, or in a campaign or expedition for which a campaign medal has been authorized and would not have been the basis for an other than honorable or general discharge.

Mothers of disabled or deceased veterans may also use this derived preference if they meet specific criteria.

Hiring Reform: Making It Easier for You to Get Hired

Having a preference or hiring authority on your side is helpful, but it isn't always enough to help you get hired in some locations. Thanks to a hiring reform initiative launched in May 2010, the federal government has done the following to simplify the hiring process:

- The cumbersome job application form has been ditched for the resume and an optional cover letter. If you are old enough to remember the multi-page application form, you'll appreciate the significance of this move. It was recently reported that 91% of positions were filled based on resumes and cover letters.
- Ninety-six percent of job announcements no longer require Knowledge, Skills and Abilities (KSAs), the narrative essay style questions that sparked fear in the hearts and minds of many applicants; however, some agencies still require them at some point in the process. It is possible that KSAs may be reincarnated under a different name in the future.
- Job announcements – 86% of them in fact – have been posted in a more reader-friendly format, with 66% consisting of five or fewer pages.

- And finally, believe it or not, the government reports hiring times for new employees have been reduced from 130 days to 105 days.

Locating Federal Jobs

You can find out about federal employment opportunities by going online and visiting USA Jobs (www.usajobs.com). It is the U.S. government's official system for federal jobs and employment information.

If you're serious about landing a federal job, then you need to regularly check out the available positions posted on this site. You can make this easy for yourself by setting up an automated search agent on the site. The jobs you've requested will then be emailed to you on a periodic basis you establish. It doesn't get any easier than that.

In theory, that should be enough. In practice, it isn't always.

Sometimes jobs, at least in the DoD world, don't seem to make it to www.usajobs.com and instead show up only on the individual service branch site. Just to be safe, you should check the service sites also:

- Department of the Army   www.armycivilianservice.com
- U.S. Air Force   www.afciviliancareers.com
- Department of the U.S. Navy   https://chart.donhr.navy.mil
- U.S. Marine Corps   www.usajobs.gov and https://chart.donhr.navy.mil

If you are by chance targeting a job within the Department of the Army, you can get even more job information from the Fully Automated System for Classification (FASCLASS): https://acpol2.army.mil/fasclass/inbox/.

For all federal positions, classifications standards and job grading system information can be found at www.opm.gov/fedclass/html.

Another useful online resource for securing federal employment is Avue Central (www.avuecentral.com).

Finding out about jobs that are already public knowledge is one thing. Finding out about jobs that have not yet been announced is something else. To enhance your chances of landing a federal job, you'll want to walk both sides of that street, so to speak.

You'll want to apply for the open jobs, and you will want to network with employers, friends, and other contacts about jobs that may or will open in the future. It's called laying the groundwork for future opportunities. It's called covering your bases. Whatever you want to call it is irrelevant. Just do it.

Applying for Federal Jobs

Let's assume you have located an already announced opportunity that you want to apply for. How do you proceed?

Once you've spotted a job that you're interested in, you need to apply for it, usually by submitting your application online.

When you apply for job opportunities, you will need a resume. You can use the USA Jobs Resume Builder and fill the blanks as you go, or you can draft one separately and upload it. To use the Resume Builder, you will need to first create an account. Go to www.usajobs.gov and click on the My Account option and follow the prompts.

Either way is painful. There is no getting around the necessity of writing a resume. Since you have to suffer through the creation of your resume one way or another, you might as well take the time to get it right on your first try.

To minimize the pain and trauma, here are 10 tips:

1. **Read the announcement carefully.** Before you spend precious time fretting over the resume and future federal job, read the job announcement word for word. Make sure you are eligible to apply for it in the first place. Note the open period and the type of position.

2. **Write to impress.** Use everyday words that concisely and professionally communicate your skills. If you want to impress, use keywords (see #4 below).

3. **Go long.** Or at least don't try to keep your resume short. Federal resumes often extend to four or more pages. If there is a preferred length, it will be given on the job announcement. Be sure you provide complete and accurate contact information and accomplishment-based work narratives.

4. **Embrace keywords.** Know them. Love them. Use them. They work. Go over the job vacancy announcement carefully and identify the buzzwords that pop up under the "requirements," "skills," or "qualifications" sections and then use them in your resume.

5. **Prioritize the information.** As you create your work narratives, put the critical information up front. Employers give a resume, even a federal one, a mere 20- to 30-second chance to pass the dreaded "keep or trash" test. Your immediate goal is have your resume be kept for further consideration.

6. **Quantify your accomplishments.** Numbers are revealing. They tell an employer just how much of an impact you made, whether it was in the number of reports you had to generate, the number of people you supervised, or the number of dollars you managed. Plug them in wherever you can to show the scope and depth of your experience.

7. **Be consistent in formatting.** If you use all capital letters when you type your job title on one entry, do the same on all the entries. However, don't use all capital letters to type your narratives unless you want to annoy the employer. NO ONE LIKES TO READ IN CAPITAL LETTERS FOR VERY LONG. Make sure there are no misspelled words or grammatical errors.

8. **Remember your goal.** You want to land a specific job, so make your resume as perfect a match for it as you can honestly do so. Compare your finished resume with the job vacancy announcement when you're finished.

9. **Think whole package.** A resume may not be all that you are required to submit in order to be considered for the job. You may

have to complete a questionnaire, or you could be asked to submit a set of KSAs even though technically "they are no longer required." But you know all this. You carefully read the job vacancy announcement. *Right?*

10. **Have a back-up plan.** You might luck in to a federal job when you want it. You might not. Have a Plan B ready in any event. If you need to work or will simply go crazy without a job, then be prepared to accept other employment that may not be your first choice but does provide a paycheck and will hold you over until a better job comes along.

Locating and applying for federal employment can be a daunting task, but you don't have to go it alone. Take advantage of the expert and free services available at any military family support center's employment readiness program.

The Front Door/Back Door Approach

You want a federal job. You know how to locate them and how to apply for them. You've been there, done that, and pushed the "Submit" button on more than one occasion. Now, you are just sitting back and waiting for the telephone calls and interviews sure to come.

If only it were so simple.

When you are applying for a non-federal job in the civilian world, you know that **networking** is key. You know that you have to reach out and connect with potential employers about opportunities within their organizations.

It's no different in the federal world, but many applicants somehow fail to see it that way. Sure, your application has to meet certain requirements. That's a given. Don't make the critical error, however, of thinking that the traditional concept of networking doesn't apply here.

As you identify federal job opportunities, work to establish a "back door" relationship in the process. Meet the employer. See if there is an option to schedule an "information interview" with him or her to learn more about the position before you apply for it.

When you conduct an information interview, you not only learn more information about the job and the agency than is given on the announcement, but now you become a known candidate.

Employers are more likely to take a second, closer look at your application if they already know you and know that you are interested in the job.

You become more than just a name on a referral list. You become **real**!

6

Writing a Resume Employers Will Love

IT'S UNDERSTANDABLE IF the thought of creating or revising a resume terrifies you. It probably should.

Think about it. Decisions are made based on its appearance and content. Studies show that employers only look at a resume, initially at least, for 20 to 30 seconds. In that short period of time, they decide to either keep it for a more detailed read or pitch it.

Let's be clear. You want your resume to be a keeper. You want an employer's interest to be peaked enough to invite you in for that coveted face-to-face interview.

To accomplish this, your resume has to be more than good. It has to stand out from the others in a positive manner. It has to be written with the employer in mind rather than with you in mind. It is not a "love me" document that you write for your own ego.

The good news? You don't have to be an expert to write an effective resume that stands out. You can do it yourself if you put in the time and effort. It doesn't hurt to have patience and caffeine nearby either.

Four Easy Steps to Creating a Good Resume

A competitive resume is within your reach if you follow these four easy steps.

STEP 1: Choose an appropriate resume format.

STEP 2: Outline the resume, without detailed content.

STEP 3: Add the detailed, targeted content to the resume.

STEP 4: Review and revise, review and revise (you can't do this too often!)

Now for the down and dirty details you need to know to make it happen.

STEP 1: Choose an appropriate resume format.

Typically, resumes are created in one of the following three formats:

Chronological format: This is a date-centered resume where your most recent work experience is listed first and you work backwards in time showing from five to ten years worth of jobs. Employers often prefer this format over others.

Use the chronological format when:

- You have worked consistently from year to year, without significant time gaps between jobs.
- You have worked in the same job or industry for several years and your resume will show progression through the ranks.
- A potential employer requests it.

Avoid using the chronological format when:

- You are trying to switch into a different job or industry.
- You are re-entering the workforce after an extended absence.
- You have significant time gaps between jobs.

Functional format: This is a skills-based resume that focuses on your areas of expertise rather than on your work history. Some employers say they do not like this format as much as the others because it doesn't contain a work history.

Use the functional format when:

- You are switching into a different job or industry.
- You have significant time gaps between jobs.
- You are re-entering the work after an extended absence.

Avoid using the functional format when you have a consistent work history in one job area and want to stay in that area.

Combination format: This resume takes the best features from both the chronological and functional resume formats. It typically highlights skills and abilities first and then provides the employer with your work history.

Use the combination format when:

- You want to de-emphasize your work history but not exclude it completely.
- You are switching into a different job or industry.

Avoid using the combination format when:

- You have a consistent work history and you are targeting similar jobs to what you have done in the past.

Decide on one format of resume to use right now. You can always create a different format later, but focus on one format at a time.

STEP 2: Outline the resume, without detailed content.

Once you have decided which format to use, it will be helpful to prepare a basic outline. Doing so allows you to get an overall structural feel for what the resume will end up looking like when you're finished.

The completed outline provides you with a glimmer of light at the end of the resume-writing tunnel.

Glimmers of light are encouraging.

Now, let's look at each of the format types again, identifying how to outline them and what content can easily be added to each section at this point.

The **chronological resume format** will include these items:

- **Heading.** This should be at the top of the page, with a one-inch margin from the edge of the document. It should include your name, address, and contact information. The formatting of the heading could match the formatting of the heading on the accompanying cover letter for a nice effect. (More about cover letters in Chapter 7.) You can center the heading or justify it to the left or right of the page.

- **Objective Statement.** This is a one- or two-liner that focuses the attention of the resume on one job or industry. Every line on the resume should directly or indirectly support it. It should not be vague. It should be specific.

  Here are a few sample objective statements:

  A position as a special event coordinator within the defense industry

  Management position working within a nonprofit organization

  Customer Care Representative for XYZ Company

  Notice that the wording and presentation can vary. You can be relatively vague without sacrificing focus by indicating the basic job title you are seeking. You can also zero in on the job and the industry or even on the job and a specific company. As a general rule, remember that the more specific your objective statement, the better.

  What you should avoid in an objective statement is using too many words that say nothing substantial. For example:

  A position where I can use my proven skills to make a bold difference for your organization

  Don't make the employer have to try to figure you out. You want him to know right away exactly what your job objective is, so he or she can move on to read about your skills and experiences, which you've highlighted below the objective statement.

- **Summary of Qualifications.** In five to ten lines, you provide a brief overview of your qualifications. Consider this the "movie trailer" version of your resume.

  For example, you could include the number of years experience you have in a given area, any particular skills or abilities that you have that are required for the job, and specific credentials (licenses or certifications) that are relevant to the position.

Also, note that you don't have to call this section a "Summary of Qualifications," if you don't want to. You may want to title it "Professional Profile" or simply "Summary."

- **Work Experience.** In the chronological format, this is where you list your most recent job title, employer, and from/to dates, along with an experience narrative. There is no hard and fast rule regarding how far back you should go here, but five to ten years is generally the accepted parameter used. Leave enough space here to go back and fill in the details later.

- **Education/Training.** In this section of a resume, you want to list the most recent and most relevant education and training you've completed. If you are currently enrolled in coursework, you want to reflect that as well. You don't want this section to turn into a long list of every class you've completed. Keep it current and keep it relevant.

An example of a **chronological outline format** can be found on page 99.

> Once you've written your resume, keep it updated. It should be a living, breathing document that you never have to endure starting from scratch again to create.

The **functional resume format** will include these items:

- **Heading.** The same guidance applies here as it does for the chronological format above. The heading should be at the top of the page, with a one-inch margin from the edge of the document. It should include your name, address, and contact information. The formatting of the heading could match the formatting of the heading on the accompanying cover letter for a nice effect. (More about cover letters in Chapter 7.) You can center the heading or justify it to the left or right of the page.

- **Objective Statement.** This is a one- or two-liner that focuses the attention of the resume on one job or industry. Every line on the resume should directly or indirectly support it. It should not be vague.

It should be specific. See the previous examples and discussion provided on page 100 for more guidance.

- **Summary of Qualifications.** The content of the summary will be the same for the functional format as it is for the chronological format. In five to ten lines, you provide a brief overview of your qualifications.

  For example, you could include the number of years experience you have in a given area, any particular skills or abilities that you have that are required for the job, and specific credentials (licenses or certifications) that are relevant to the position.

  Also, as previously noted, you don't have to call this section a "Summary of Qualifications," if you don't want to. You may want to title it "Professional Profile" or simply "Summary."

- **Areas of Expertise.** This is where you see the difference between the chronological and functional formats. Instead of launching into a work history, you launch into your areas of expertise. These are the three to five skill areas that you want the employer to know most about.

- **Education/Training.** In this section of a resume, you want to list the most recent and most relevant education and training you've completed. Again, if you are currently enrolled in coursework, you want to reflect that as well. You don't want this section to turn into a long list of every class you've completed. Keep it current and keep it relevant.

An example of a **functional outline format** can be found on page 104.

The **combination resume format** will include these items:

- **Heading.** Once again, ditto the guidance. The heading should be at the top of the page, with a one-inch margin from the edge of the document. It should include your name, address, and contact information. The formatting of the heading could match the formatting of the heading on the accompanying cover letter for a nice effect. (More about cover letters in Chapter 7.) You can center the heading or justify it to the left or right of the page.

- **Objective Statement.** Following the same guidelines as provided above for the other formats, the objective statement is a one- or two-liner that focuses the attention of the resume on one job or industry. Every line on the resume should directly or indirectly support it. It should not be vague. It should be specific.

- **Summary of Qualifications.** Once again, in five to ten lines, you provide a brief overview of your qualifications.

  For example, you could include the number of years experience you have in a given area, any particular skills or abilities that you have that are required for the job, and specific credentials (licenses or certifications) that are relevant to the position.

  Also, note that you don't have to call this section a "Summary of Qualifications," if you don't want to. You may want to title it "Professional Profile" or simply "Summary."

- **Areas of Expertise.** Here again is where you see the difference between the chronological and functional formats. Instead of launching into a work history, you launch into your areas of expertise. These are the three to five skill areas that you want the employer to know most about.

- **Work History.** In the combination format, you can provide your work history, without experience narratives, after the Areas of Expertise section.

- **Education/Training.** And finally, as in the above education and training sections, you want to list the most recent and most relevant education and training you've completed. If you are currently enrolled in coursework, you want to reflect that as well. You don't want this section to turn into a long list of every class you've completed. Keep it current and keep it relevant.

An example of a **combination outline format** can be found on page 108.

STEP 3: Add the detailed, targeted content to the resume.

You've selected an appropriate resume format and you have prepared a basic outline. Now it's time to go back and fill up all those blank spaces with detailed and relevant content. *Relevant* is a key word here.

If you are creating your resume for the purpose of applying for a specific job or for a specific type of job, then do your best to match your skills with what the employer seeks.

The first time you draft this, just get it down in words. Don't edit or criticize any first attempt. There will be plenty of time for that later, in Step 4.

Remember the following as you add your content to the outline:

- **Resume sentences are strange.** They are not written in first person using I. Resume sentences begin with an action verb and end with something you did.

  For example, the following sentence doesn't belong on your resume: **I supervised employees.**

  It is better to write: **Supervised five employees.**

  The "I" is dropped, as it is understood without writing it and we now know that you supervised five employees. You are the understood subject in the sentences of your resume.

  It is even better to write: **Effectively supervised five employees working in a customer service department.**

  Now we're getting somewhere. We know that you're an effective supervisor of five people and those people worked in a customer service department.

- **Use numbers.** By providing numbers, such as in the example above, you give the employer a better idea of what you did and, by extension, what you may be capable of doing in the future. Giving dollar amounts, or number of people supervised or served, provides a clearer picture of the scope of your accomplishments.

  If you start a sentence with a number, capitalize it as you spell it out. If a number falls somewhere in the sentence and not at the beginning, spell it out if it is nine or below. Ten and above can be written in numerals and not as words.

- **Cite your accomplishments.** Don't let your work experience narratives or areas of expertise sound like basic job descriptions. That's not the point to creating the resume. Instead, focus on what you have actually accomplished on the job or in a skill area. Push that instead of what you were responsible for doing. To expand your narratives even further, ask yourself how you did something and write about it.

- **Avoid repetitive wording.** It's acceptable to use the same words over and over again in the first draft of your resume. You are just trying to develop an idea at that point and it's fine to use whatever words you need. In the second draft, however, you must banish repetitive wording.

  Case in point: *"Responsible for..."* is one of the biggest offenders. First of all, it is too passive for a sentence beginning. Better to start the sentence with a power verb (see page 93 for a list of power verbs). Second, it is weak when used even once. Used more than once in the same narrative, it comes across as just plain lazy. Don't be lazy. You're so much better than that.

- **Be careful with capitalization.** You've been around the military long enough to know that if it seems important, it should be capitalized. However, that rule doesn't apply to your resume. Let the real rules of English prevail here.

- **See Words You Can Use in Your Resume** on page 93 for potential power verbs and functional skills headings.

- **From/To Dates.** Include the month and the years if you don't have any breaks of time in employment. If you have gaps in the months but not in the years, just use from/to years instead. If you have big gaps in both, either use a functional format resume and eliminate the employment history altogether, or use a combination format resume and indicate number of years experience rather than give a from/to period.

STEP 4: Review and revise, review and revise.

Congratulations! You've made it through three of the four steps by now. You deserve a little R&R. No, not the fun kind of R&R we all look forward to, but the Review & Revise kind. The fun kind comes later, when you're employed and can afford it. For now, you must suffer through this final step.

After the resume is drafted, it's time to go back over it yet again. Read it with an objective eye. Be brutal and make corrections you feel are warranted to enhance its effectiveness.

After that, go a step further. Ask a trusted colleague, mentor, or networking contact who is familiar with the job requirements to also review it for you and give you their feedback.

Once you've made any other revisions to your resume, bounce it against the Smart Job Choices Resume checklist on page 97 for one final review before sending it to an employer.

Resume writing can seem complicated because there is more than one way to write one.
Stick to the plan and you'll get it done.

Words You Can Use in Your Resume

Power Verbs: Effective Resume Sentence Starters

acted	arbitrated	authored
adapted	arranged	balanced
addressed	assembled	budgeted
administered	assessed	built
advised	assigned	calculated
analyzed	assisted	chaired
appraised	attained	clarified
approved	audited	coached

collaborated
collected
communicated
compiled
computed
conceptualized
consolidated
contracted
convenience
coordinated
corresponded
counseled
created
customized
delegated
demonstrated
designed
developed
devised
diagnosed
directed
dispatched
drafted
edited
educated
enabled
encouraged
engineered
enlisted
evaluated
examined
executed
expanded
expedited
explained
extracted

fabricated
facilitated
familiarized
fashioned
forecasted
formulated
founded
generated
guided
identified
illustrated
implemented
improved
increased
influenced
informed
initiated
inspected
instituted
instructed
integrated
interpreted
interviewed
introduced
invented
investigated
lectured
maintained
managed
marketed
mediated
moderated
monitored
motivated
negotiated
operated

organized
originated
overhauled
oversaw
performed
persuaded
pioneered
planned
prepared
prioritized
processed
produced
programmed
projected
promoted
publicized
purchased
recommended
reconciled
recorded
recruited
reduced
referred
rehabilitated
remodeled
repaired
represented
researched
restored
retrieved
reviewed
revitalized
scheduled
screened
shaped
solved

spearheaded	supervised	transformed
specified	surveyed	translated
spokc	systematized	upgraded
stimulated	systemized	validated
strengthened	tabulated	wrote
summarized	trained	

For the Functional/Combination Resumes: Functional Skill Headings

Note: You can also convert these headings into job titles and use them instead.

Account Management	Distribution Management
Accounting	Drama
Acquisition	Driving
Administration	Engineering
Advertising	Evaluation
Analysis and Evaluation	Event Planning
Artist	Family Advocacy
Banking	Field Research
Blogging	Film and Video
Bookkeeping	Financial Management
Business Management	Financial Planning
Career Counseling	Food Preparation
Career Development	Forecasting
Child Care	Graphic Design
Coaching	Hair Styling
Collections	Health Care
Community Relations	Home Health Care
Community Support	Hospitality
Content Development	Human Resources
Cook	Human Services
Cosmetology	Information Technology
Customer Service	Inspection
Database Management	Installation
Design	Instruction
Directing	Insurance
Dispatch	Intelligence

Interior Design	Public Affairs
International Relations	Public Relations
Interviewing	Publicity
Inventory Control	Purchasing
Investigation	Real Estate
Labor Relations	Recruiting
Legal Assistance	Reporting
Logistics Management	Restaurant Management
Maintenance	Retail Management
Management	Safety
Management Analysis	Sales
Market Research	Security
Material Handling	Social Work
Material Management	Staffing
Mechanics	Statistical Analysis
Media	Statistics
Mediation	Supervision
Medical Billing	Supply
Medical Transcription	Systems Administration
Mental Health	Tax Preparation
Merchandising	Teaching
Multimedia	Technical Writing
Negotiation	Telecommunications
Network Administration	Theatre Production
Nursing	Therapy
Nutrition	Training
Office Management	Translator
Organizational Planning	Veterinary Technician
Personal Training	Virtual Assistance
Personnel	Volunteer Management
Photography	Website Design
Plans and Policy	Website Maintenance
Program Management	Wellness
Project Management	Workforce Development
Protocol	Writing

RESUME CHECKLIST

The Heading:
❏ Your name, address, telephone, and email address are provided.
❏ Your name, address, telephone, and email address are correctly typed.

Objective Statement:
❏ A clear and concise objective statement is provided.

Summary of Qualifications:
❏ One is provided that offers the employer a brief and targeted overview of the resume.

Work or Skill Narratives:
❏ Each line supports the objective, whether objective is stated on resume or not.
❏ Quantified accomplishment-based statements are used.
❏ Resume shows a clear match between the job you seek and your skills/qualifications.
❏ Resume uses the language of the industry being targeted.
❏ Repetitive words or phrases are avoided.
❏ First person singular (I) is avoided.
❏ Power verbs and descriptive skill headings are used throughout.

Work History:
❏ Job titles are listed first before employer, location, and dates of employment.
❏ From/To year dates are used and do not emphasize time gaps.

Layout and Appearance:
❏ Resume looks professional, with a 1- to 1.5-inch margin on top, bottom, and sides.
❏ An 11- or 12-point font (Times New Roman or Arial) is used.
❏ No distracting use or abuse of italics, underlines, caps, or bolding in the resume.
❏ There are no spelling or grammatical errors.

Resume Example 1: Before

Sandra Wagner
CMR 480 Box 5555
APO AE 09131
(49) 5555-555-55555

> Incomplete heading that does not stand out.

Employment History

Robinson Barracks Elementary/Middle School PTSA
Stuttgart, Germany
President, June 2010 – June 2011

> Employer and location given more emphasis than job seeker.

Responsible for running the PTSA monthly board meetings and quarterly general membership meetings to include creating meeting agendas. Maintained the PTSA calendar by working closely with the school administration to coordinate dates and events. Monitored fundraising events that brought in over $10,000. Represented the PTSA in various school and community-wide events.

Creekside Elementary School
Milledgeville, GA
Special Education Paraprofessional, October 2007 – May 2009

Worked in the classroom with special needs students in grades 2, 3, and 4. Helped to modify teacher lessons to suit the learning styles of the students. Also worked with students individually and in a smaller classroom setting in differentiated instruction.

Home Management
February 1997 – September 2007

Central Texas College
Baumholder, Germany
Registrar, June 1995 – January 1997

> - Repetitive wording and a lack of clarity.
> - Work narratives shortchange job seeker.
> - Functional/Combo could be better format.
> - Chronological goes back too far here.
> - Layout/font sizes need adjusting.

Responsible for registering students for classes, ordering books, and coordinating assignment of classrooms. **Responsible for** advertising class offerings and descriptions. Filed reports to higher headquarters as well as the Baumholder Education Center.

Impostors
Savannah, GA
Manager, July 1991 – August 1993

Responsible for the day to day operations of a franchise store. **Responsible for** hiring and training employees as well as marketing and advertising. Attended quarterly buying sessions in California as well as restocking inventory on a monthly basis.

Law Office of Debbie Bolan
North Andover, MA
Paraprofessional, June 1990 – July 1991

Responsible for all collection cases. Maintained files, issued official collection letters, filed collection cases in local courts.

Education

University of New Hampshire
Durham, NH
B.A., Sociology, 1990

> Degree buried here.

Resume Example 1: After

SANDRA WAGNER

CMR 480, Box 5555, APO AE 09131   From USA: 011-49-555-555-55555
APO AE 09131   From Germany: 0711-555-55555
swagner@email.com

Summary of Qualifications

A dedicated and caring professional with extensive experience in special education and school administration. Extremely organized and results-oriented individual who is able to work effectively with diverse groups. Exceptional negotiating skills. Highly creative and flexible. Proficient in MS Office. Solid organizational, financial, and volunteer management skills.

Work Experience

President, Parent Teacher Student Association (PTSA)   2010 – 2011
Robinson Barracks Elementary/Middle School, Stuttgart, Germany

Elected to serve as school association president for a one-year term. Established and managed the objectives and strategies of a PTSA in Europe. Recruited and supervised 20+ committee chairs and 100+ volunteers. Oversaw a $50k budget, ensuring accurate accountability and use of funds. Monitored fundraising events that raised over $10k. Kept parents, students, and faculty informed about calendar events and PTSA accomplishments. Represented the PTSA in school and community events. Created agenda and led monthly executive board meetings and quarterly general membership meetings. Served as mediator between parties resolving conflicts when necessary. Maintained the PTSA calendar by working closely with the school administration to coordinate dates and events.

Special Education Paraprofessional   2007 – 2009
Creekside Elementary School, Milledgeville, Georgia

Worked closely with teachers, administrators, and parents of special needs students in grades 2-4 to reinforce learning materials. Modified teacher lessons to suit the learning styles of the students. Assisted students individually and in a smaller classroom setting in differentiated instruction. Monitored student work and corrected papers. Answered student questions and served as trusted point of contact for them throughout the school day. Supervised students during recess, lunch periods, and on field trips.

Education

Bachelor of Arts, Sociology, University of New Hampshire, Durham, New Hampshire

Notes About Sandra's Resume

In this example, Sandra is a military spouse stationed in Germany and wants to apply for jobs in the U.S. where she will soon be PCS'ing. She doesn't have a specific job that she is applying for, but she wants to develop a basic resume now which she can target further as she applies for education-related opportunities.

In her first draft here ("before" version), she has chosen to use a chronological format. As it is, this version goes too far back in time and puts too much emphasis on her period of unemployment as represented by "Home Management." Changes need to be made to eliminate that emphasis.

Here are more comments about the "before" and "after" differences:

- In the "before" version, the **heading** lacks an email address and clarity about the telephone number. In this case, Sandra is targeting employers in the U.S. and she lives in Germany. Stateside employers are not always familiar with how to call someone overseas. By providing more specific guidance, she will be more able to receive a call. If not a call, at least an email is possible if the address is given. On the "after" version of the resume, the heading is revised to reflect these changes.

- There is no **Objective Statement** or **Summary of Qualifications** on the "before" resume. On the "after" resume, an objective was not included, as Sandra is not applying for a specific job yet, but she is targeting a specific area. In the added summary of qualifications on the "after" version, the employer can now quickly see more information about her skills and abilities.

  As she applies for specific jobs, she can target the resume even further in these areas.

- In the "after" version, the **work experience** section has been completely overhauled. The older experiences, including Home Management, have been deleted. That is not done to minimize the importance of that experience, but rather to focus on her current and consistent work history since it supports what she currently wants to do.

The oft-repeated words "responsible for" are deleted. The work narratives of the remaining history shown on the "after" version are expanded. Numbers are used to quantify her accomplishments. The months are omitted from the From/To time periods.

- In the **Education** block, her degree is spelled out and the year earned is eliminated to minimize emphasis on her age.

- Layout-wise, the "after" resume has been edited as well. The font was changed to Times New Roman for the majority of the text. Her name was bolded and typed in a 14-point size for added emphasis. The address and contact information was typed in a 10-point size in order to put more attention on her name. The remainder of the document headings were typed in 12-point, again drawing the eye to them. Employers and locations were italicized in a 10-point font while her job titles were bolded in an 11-point font size, again drawing more attention to her job title (and by extension her) rather than on her past employers and locations.

More Food for Thought

Sandra can further improve this revised version of the resume, targeting it specifically to the jobs for which she actually applies.

She could also easily adapt this resume to a functional or combination format resume. Doing so would allow her to show an employer some of that past work experience that was omitted in this chronological format.

If she is interested in working in another franchise or administrative office, it would be to her advantage to create the different version.

You can have more than one format of resume. Different opportunities may call for it.

Don't make the mistake of writing your resume for yourself. It may be about you, but it is written for a potential employer.

Resume Example 2: Before

> Delete "email" and "telephone."
> Nice layout.

Theresa Taylor Smith
5555 Mulberry Run Lane, Fairfax, VA 22030
Email: ttsmith@email.com; Telephone: (555) 555-5555

SUMMARY OF QUALIFICATIONS
- Over 10 years of experience in coordinating events, itineraries, and agendas
- Postgraduate, certified training in protocol and etiquette
- Easily develops rapport with civilians, military personnel, and distinguished visitors
- Retains personal library of 125+ protocol and etiquette reference books for research
- Poised, well-organized, and dedicated; able to meet deadlines
- "Clearable," able to obtain and maintain security clearances [move clearances to above line]

AREAS OF EXPERTISE
Event Coordinator

> -Some time gap and spacing issues.
> -Good use of numbers throughout.

Vice-President of Programs
Protestant Women of the Chapel
United States Army Garrison-Stuttgart, Germany
August 2010-Present

- Created annual event schedule and monthly agendas within a limited budget
- Developed monthly themes, menu selections, and table/room decorations
- Coordinated two large-scale, kick-off events comprising 40+ guests and staff
- Projected expenses for upcoming events and submitted monthly activity reports

Event Coordinator
Advanced Airlift Tactics Training Center
139th Airlift Wing, Rosecrans Air National Guard; St. Joseph, MO
February 2003-September 2009

- Provided hospitality support for official promotion and retirement ceremonies
- Advised 2009 Symposium Committee with dinner party arrangements for distinguished visitors
- Coordinated and hosted 2004 holiday Staff Dinner in historic home for 50+ guests
- Organized countless spouses' social and support functions
- Provided on-site administrative and communication support to the 139th Airlift Wing Family Readiness Group during deployments and base-wide activities in 2003-2005

Etiquette Consultant
Beyond Charm, Etiquette & Image Consulting, L.L.C.
St. Joseph, MO
May 2007-June 2009

- Formulated credible, small business plan; managed office space and monthly expenditures
- Developed annual schedule and budget for instructional classes and group events

Theresa Taylor Smith
Page 2

- Established creative marketing strategies such personal website, online question-naires, gift referrals, and social networking
- Assessed and amended clientele's correspondence and itineraries
- Coordinated five-course dining events for community groups utilizing "enter-train-ment" techniques
- Attained personal library of 125+ etiquette and protocol reference books for continuing education and research

Event Coordinator and Facilitator
Green Valley Baptist Church
St. Joseph, MO
May 2005-May 2007

- Directed a 10+ volunteer staff to procure a two-day women's retreat with a key-note speaker and hospitality for 50+ participants in 2007
- Selected to attend the 2006 LifeWay's National Women's Ministry Forum in Nashville, TN
- Coordinated and hosted two annual seven-course dinners to honor the staff in 2005 and 2006
- Co-facilitated women's weekly group studies consisting of 12+ members over a two-year period

EDUCATION AND CERTIFICATION

Fundamentals of Protocol
Do-it-Right Protocol; Scotsdale, AZ
December 2007, 28 Hours; www.doitrightprotocol.com

> Misspelled city name.

Principles of Etiquette
The American School of Protocol; Atlanta, GA
April 2007, 40 Hours; www.theamericanschoolofprotocol.com

Hardin-Simmons University
B.S., Applied Theology; Abilene, TX
1996; www.hsutx.edu

> Spell out degree.

ADDITIONAL INFORMATION

Clerical Skills	**Microsoft Office/Vista Skills**	
Typing: 60+WPM	**MAC OS X Software Skills**	
Dictation: 100+WPM	Word	iWorks
10-Key	PowerPoint	iMovie
	Excel	iPhoto

> No need to high-light these skills in a separate section unless specifically noted on job announcement.

Resume Example 2: After

Theresa Taylor Smith

5555 Mulberry Run Lane, Fairfax, VA 22030 ttsmith@email.com (555) 555-5555

Objective

A position as an event planner within the defense industry or a corporate environment

Summary of Qualifications

Ten plus years experience coordinating senior management level special events within the U.S. defense community. Successfully completed extensive certified training in protocol and etiquette. Maintain reference library of 125+ resources. Poised, well organized, and dedicated. Easily develops rapport with civilians, military personnel, and distinguished visitors. Able to meet or beat deadlines. Excellent administrative skills. Able to obtain and maintain a security clearance.

Work History

Event Coordinator/Programs Vice-President   2010 – 2012
Protestant Women of the Chapel, Fort Campbell, Kentucky

- Created annual event schedule and monthly agendas within a limited budget.
- Developed monthly themes, menu selections, and table/room decorations for events.
- Coordinated two large-scale, kick-off events for 40+ guests and staff.
- Projected expenses for upcoming events and prepared monthly activity reports.

Event Coordinator   2003 – 2009
Rosecrans Air National Guard, St. Joseph, Missouri

- Provided hospitality support for military promotion and retirement ceremonies.
- Served as protocol advisor to major dinner party event for distinguished visitors.
- Coordinated and hosted annual holiday staff dinner in an historic home for 50+ guests.
- Organized numerous spouses' social and support functions.
- Provided on-site administrative and communication support to family readiness group.

Etiquette Consultant   2007 – 2009
Beyond Charm, L.L.C., St. Joseph, Missouri

- Managed an etiquette and image consulting business.
- Developed annual schedule and budget for instructional classes and group events.
- Established attention-getting creative marketing strategies.
- Reviewed and amended clientele's correspondence and itineraries for correctness.
- Coordinated five-course dining events for groups utilizing "enter-*train*-ment" techniques.

Theresa Taylor Smith – Page 2

Event Coordinator/Facilitator   2005 – 2007
Green Valley Baptist Church, St. Joseph, Missouri

- Directed 10+ volunteers in organizing events for a two-day retreat for over 50 participants.
- Selected over others to represent organization at a prestigious national event.
- Coordinated and hosted two annual seven-course dinners to honor the staff members.
- Co-facilitated women's weekly group studies consisting of 12+ members.

Education and Training

- Bachelor's Degree, Applied Theology, Hardin-Simmons University, Abilene, Texas
- Fundamentals of Protocol, 28 hours, Do-It-Right Protocol, Scottsdale, Arizona
- Principles of Etiquette, 40 hours, The American School of Protocol, Atlanta, Georgia

Notes About Theresa's Resume

In this example, Theresa is a military spouse stationed in Virginia and wants to work in event planning, an area where she has a history of experience.

The "before" version provided here is not the first draft she has written. She has worked diligently to get it to this point and it is now a good resume. At this point, she only needs to make a few minor changes to turn it into a great resume.

Here are the changes made in the "after" version that accomplishes that move from good to great:

- The **heading**, in the "before" version, is eye-catching but almost too much so. The reader's eyes move immediately to the stylistic line below her name rather than to her name. Also, the words "Email:" and "Telephone:" are unnecessary. Everyone understands what those are without the labels attached.

  In the "after" version, her name has been centered on the page and isolated from her address. Her address has been contained between two lines, making it a convenient spot for the employer to find it.

- In the "before" version, an **objective statement** is missing. It is added to the "after" version. While Theresa has a clear focus for this resume, employers will nevertheless appreciate seeing it within the first few seconds of looking at the document.

- In the "before" version, a good **summary of qualifications** is provided. The emphasis she wishes it to have, however, is lost in the bullet formatting that exactly resembles the work history blocks below. There is nothing here to make it stand out, and that's what we want it to do.

  To make the summary of qualifications stand out better, the "after" version presents it in paragraph form. As she applies for jobs, Theresa can go back to this section (and the entire resume for that matter) and tailor it more specifically to the particular position.

- The **work experience** blocks in the "before" version have good narratives that only required minor revision. Dated events such as the 2004 holiday staff dinner were generalized to communicate the ability rather than the event itself. Theresa does a good job of using power verbs and keeping her sentences concise and relevant.

As she applies for specific jobs, she should go back and expand her work narratives more specifically. For example, how did she organize numerous social and support functions? What were the tasks involved in doing that and would it be to her advantage, when applying for a specific job, to elaborate on those tasks?

The job title sections in the work experience block, however, needed help. They were far too crowded in spacing and words. Take a look at how different it appears in the "after" version. Less is more.

- We condensed the **Education** block on the "after" version of her resume, eliminating the website references and dates of completion to keep consistency intact. We also spelled out the educational degree.

- Layout-wise, Theresa uses an **Arial font** with varying sizes and we continued that in the "after" version, adding italics for the employer and locations.

- Spacing of the **bullets** throughout was corrected for easier readability.

**Consistency in formatting
is golden.**

See how easily Theresa's resume can be changed into a combination format resume on the following page. A few more job details were included to expand the areas of expertise; however, most of the wording remains intact and is merely reorganized.

Theresa Taylor Smith

5555 Mulberry Run Lane, Fairfax, VA 22030 ttsmith@email.com (555) 555-5555

Objective

A position as an event planner within the defense industry or
a corporate environment

Summary of Qualifications

Ten plus years experience coordinating senior management level special events within the U.S. defense community. Successfully completed extensive certified training in protocol and etiquette. Maintain reference library of 125+ resources. Poised, well organized, and dedicated. Easily develops rapport with civilians, military personnel, and distinguished visitors. Able to meet or beat deadlines. Excellent administrative skills. Able to obtain and maintain a security clearance.

Areas of Expertise

Event Planning

- Developed monthly themes, menu selections, and table/room decorations for events.
- Coordinated two large-scale, kick-off events for 40+ guests and staff.
- Projected expenses for upcoming events and prepared monthly activity reports.
- Coordinated and hosted annual holiday staff dinner in an historic home for 50+ guests.
- Organized numerous spouses' social and support functions.
- Coordinated five-course dining events for groups utilizing "enter-train-ment" techniques.
- Established attention-getting creative marketing strategies.
- Directed 10+ volunteers in organizing events for a two-day retreat for over 50 participants.
- Coordinated and hosted two annual seven-course dinners to honor the staff members.

Protocol

- Managed an etiquette and image consulting business, meeting needs of diverse clientele.
- Provided hospitality support for military promotion and retirement ceremonies.
- Created rank and position specific seating charts for various sized functions.

Theresa Taylor Smith – Page 2

- Served as protocol advisor for major dinner party event for distinguished visitors.
- Ensured appropriate procedures for taking RSVPs from guests in place.
- Ensured biographical sketches of guests and speakers were distributed in timely manner.
- Advised and assisted in flag placement arrangements.

Administration

- Created annual event schedule and monthly agendas within a limited budget.
- Provided on-site administrative and communication support to family readiness group.
- Developed annual schedule and budget for instructional classes and group events.
- Reviewed and amended clientele's correspondence and itineraries for correctness.
- Selected over others to represent organization at a prestigious national event.
- Co-facilitated women's weekly group studies consisting of 12+ members.

Education and Training

- Bachelor's Degree, Applied Theology, Hardin-Simmons University, Abilene, Texas
- Fundamentals of Protocol, 28 hours, Do-It-Right Protocol, Scottsdale, Arizona
- Principles of Etiquette, 40 hours, The American School of Protocol, Atlanta, Georgia

Work History

Event Coordinator/Programs Vice-President   2010 – 2012
Protestant Women of the Chapel, Fort Campbell, Kentucky

Etiquette Consultant   2007 – 2009
Beyond Charm, L.L.C., St. Joseph, Missouri

Event Coordinator   2003 – 2009
Rosecrans Air National Guard, St. Joseph, Missouri

Event Coordinator/Facilitator   2005 – 2007
Green Valley Baptist Church, St. Joseph, Missouri

7

Attention-Grabbing Cover Letters

MAKING SMART JOB choices will be impossible without clearly communicating your intentions and qualifications. You do this in a number of ways throughout your job search, and one way is through crafting an attention-grabbing cover letter that accompanies your resume.

A cover letter is often defined as a letter that introduces your resume to the employer. While that's true, it's not a complete definition. The cover letter can do much more than merely refer to an attached resume for a particular job opportunity.

A cover letter, unlike a resume, can give the employer a brief glimpse of how you express yourself as a person. This is important because employers want to hire qualified people whom they can **like**. You have a great opportunity to come across as a **qualified and likable person** within the cover letter. Take advantage of it.

Writing it doesn't have to be difficult, either.

The truth is that cover letters are important and don't always get the attention they deserve. Job seekers often assume that it is a meaningless cover sheet and thus spend too little time writing one. Making such an assumption is a big mistake.

For one job opening, employers may receive hundreds of resumes and accompanying cover letters. Every cover letter received may or may not get a full read, because of the sheer volume. You just don't know, and that's all the more reason to make yours stand out from the pack.

Here are some facts you need to know about a cover letter:

- It is a letter that you send along with your resume to a potential employer that explains why you are contacting him and hopefully entices him to look over your resume.

- It is **not** a repeat of your resume in a letter format.
- It is best kept to **one page** so the employer's attention will shift to your resume faster.
- It is an opportunity for an employer to "hear your voice."

> **Always address the cover letter to a real person. If you don't know whom to send it to, make the extra effort to find out.**

Four Easy Steps to Writing a Cover Letter

Again, creating a cover letter doesn't have to be difficult. You can easily make it a challenging, nail-biting activity but there's no need if you follow these four easy steps to writing one:

STEP 1: Know your purpose.

STEP 2: Outline the basic structure, minus the main body content.

STEP 3: Add the main body content to the letter.

STEP 4: Review and revise, review and revise.

Now, let's look at each step in more detail:

STEP 1: Know your purpose.

What are you trying to accomplish by writing this cover letter?

- Are you applying for a specific job and sending the letter to an employer, along with your resume, for consideration of that job?
- Are you sending your resume, with the letter, to someone so they can have it on file in the event a position should open up?

Whatever your main purpose, know it before you even start writing. It will directly influence what you say and how you say it.

STEP 2: Outline the basic structure, minus the main body content.

Once you know the main purpose of your cover letter, you can begin to outline it. Forget about the meaty content at this point. It will only stress you out. Instead, create a skeleton structure of what the final document will look like.

A cover letter should have the following elements in it:

- **Heading.** This should be at the top of the page, with a one-inch margin from the edge of the document. It should include your name, address, and contact information such as a telephone number and an email address. The formatting of the heading could match the heading on the accompanying resume for a nice effect.

- **Date.** Two or three lines down from the heading, you can put the date either flush left in a block style or tab it over to the right side of the page. It doesn't matter. Just make sure it looks nice. This will be the date you send the letter. Write it in a non-military format such as January 1, 2013 rather than 1/13/2013 or 1 Jan 2013.

- **To Address.** Skip down two more lines and put the name of the person you are writing to and the appropriate address.

- **Salutation.** Go down another two lines and type in your salutation line. This should read something like "Dear Mrs. Smith" and not "To Whom It May Concern" or "Dear Company Representative." Use real names, spelled correctly.

- **Main Body.** Skip one line and you are ready to strut your words. Leave space here for three to four paragraphs. Details about what to write here will be discussed in the next step.

- **Signature Block.** Somewhere near where you think the end of the letter might be, type in the following, leaving enough room for your legible signature.

  Sincerely,

  Teresa Taylor Smith

  Teresa Taylor Smith

You'll find a sample outline and an example of a finished cover letter on pages 117-118.

STEP 3: Add the main body content to the letter.

After you've outlined a basic cover letter, you are ready to go back in and add the all-important main body content to it. If possible, limit the main body to three or four paragraphs. While a longer letter is not always a deal-breaker, it is best to keep the cover letter's length to one page.

In paragraphs one to two:

Explain **why** you are writing. Since you already know the purpose of your letter, drafting the first paragraph or so should be fairly easy.

You can approach this opening in one of two ways. Either way is effective. Before deciding on an approach, consider how the reader might respond to it before selecting one option over the other.

Option 1: Be direct and succinct. Long, drawn-out introductions are often ignored anyway. If you are applying for a specific job, mention the job reference number if there is one. If name-dropping is part of your strategy for the cover letter, do it here. A typical opening with this approach may sound something like this:

Attached is my resume for your review for the position of x, job number #.

It works, but it is a no-frills, to-the-point, and predictable approach.

Option 2: Be more creative with your words, avoiding the generic opening paragraph in favor of one that reveals something about the company or about you, stepping things up a level. This one may take a few more minutes to write, but it's worth it. It shows you put some real thought into the letter and the basic communication process you are opening up.

For an example of this option in action, see the example cover letter on page 118.

In paragraphs three to four:

Show the **fit** between your skills and the job in question. Include solid examples of your experiences to further make your case. Use the same words you saw in the job announcement to express yourself. Try not to repeat your resume word for word, however.

In the closing paragraph:

Proactively close out your cover letter by determining the next step in the process. Tell the employer the exact date or time frame you will follow up on the opportunity unless you are contacted first.

STEP 4: Review and revise, review and revise.

Before you begin to review and revise, run a spell and grammar check through your letter. Now, take a short break to clear your mind for a few minutes before you go back to it. Read over it once more and consider these questions:

- How does it sound? Do the words flow easily? Does it sound professional?

- Does it show a little bit of your own personality as well? Do you come across as qualified and likable?

- Do you communicate your key information, showing a match between your skills and those required for the job you are applying for?

- Do you get to the point quickly so that the reader (employer) knows why your cover letter is in his or her hands?

Now, go back over it again, this time with a red pen. Red means you care. Care a great deal and make any notes that need to be made along the way.

- Read each word carefully and make sure the right words were used. Spelling and grammar checks are not refined enough yet to do the same job as the human eye. Read and re-read.

- Does your letter achieve the objective you had for it in the first place?

- Did you use the words that the employer already provided for you in the job announcement? There's no need to reinvent the proverbial wheel. If you have the skills the position requires, say so using the same words the employer used in the advertisement for the job.

Make any edits that are needed and then ask someone whom you trust to read over the letter and offer you an objective opinion on it.

Once you feel the letter has the right tone, appropriately targeted content, and a professional appearance, then it is ready to be sent to an employer, along with your resume.

Try drafting a cover letter. When you've finished, compare it to the Cover Letter Checklist on the next page and make revisions as necessary.

COVER LETTER DO'S AND DON'TS

Do keep your letter short, sweet, and to the point. One page is best.

Do address it to a specific person. If you don't know who that should be, find out and spell names correctly.

Do personalize the letter with your unique voice.

Do match your cover letter heading to the one on your resume.

Don't recycle your cover letters. Make each one unique to the opportunity.

Don't repeat your resume in the letter.

Don't rely on tired clichés to write your letter.

COVER LETTER CHECKLIST

The Heading:
❑ Sender's name, address, telephone, and email address are given.
❑ Sender's name, address, telephone, and email address are correctly typed.

Date:
❑ Date is correct and formatted in a "civilian" style.

To Address and Salutation Line:
❑ Address is correct and post office friendly if applicable.
❑ Letter is addressed to real person and not a job title or "to whom it may concern."
❑ Real person's name is correctly spelled.
❑ Gender-confused name issues are resolved before letter is sent.

Main Body:
❑ Letter gets to the point in the first paragraph.
❑ Job announcement number is referenced, if applicable.
❑ Letter shows a clear match between the job and your skills/qualifications.
❑ Letter uses the language of the industry being targeted.
❑ Resume is not repeated within the main body of letter.
❑ Conservational tone is used that reflects your unique voice.
❑ A proactive closing is used in the letter that sets the stage for the next step in process.

Signature Block:
❑ Letter has one and it is actually signed.

Layout and Appearance:
❑ Letter looks professional, with a 1- to 1.5-inch margin on top, bottom, and sides.
❑ An 11- or 12-point font (Times New Roman or Arial) is used.
❑ There is no distracting use or abuse of italics, underlines, caps, or bolding in the letter.
❑ There are no spelling or grammatical errors.

Sample Cover Letter Outline

Your Name
Address Line 1
Address Line 2
Telephone/Email

Date

Real Person, Job Title
Address Line 1
Address Line 2

Dear Real Person,

Paragraph One: Explain why you are writing in the first place. Reference job title and vacancy number if applicable.

Paragraph Two: Show the fit between you and the job.

Paragraph Three: Proactively close out the letter establishing the next step in the process.

Sincerely,

Your Signature

Your Printed Name

Example of a Cover Letter

Theresa Taylor Smith

5555 Mulberry Run Lane, Fairfax, VA 22030 ttsmith@email.com (555) 555-5555

June 15, 2012

Emma Bailey, Protocol Manager
ABC Defense Contracting
5555-A Gallows Road
Fairfax, Virginia 22042

Dear Mrs. Bailey,

As a leader in the defense industry, you know that details count. Left unattended, they can damage a business relationship, forfeit a contract, or reverse the hard-fought progress of a team effort. You have your area of expertise and you rely on your protocol specialists to know theirs.

As an experienced event planner within the military community, I understand the importance of getting it right, and I would like to discuss the possibility of working as a protocol specialist with your company. I understand you have an opening at the moment, Job #035-11, and I am sending my resume to you for your consideration.

As a motivated self-starter, I can bring the following attributes you seek to the job:

- A bachelor's degree
- 7+ years work experience in a military environment
- Excellent organizational and communication skills, verbal and written
- Ability to multi-task and meet deadlines with minimal oversight
- Strong attention to detail with exceptional note-taking abilities
- MS Office proficiency
- Ability to obtain a Department of Defense Security Clearance

Please see the attached resume for more information about my qualifications. I welcome the opportunity to discuss this position with you in more detail. I will contact you the week of June 25th if I haven't heard back from you first.

Thank you.

Sincerely,

Theresa Taylor Smith

Theresa Taylor Smith

8

The Job Interview:
A Conversation You Want
to be Ready For

AN EMPLOYER HAS asked you to come in for a job interview. Credit your outstanding resume, your cleverly crafted cover letter, your daily horoscope, or the friend of friend who put in a good word for you. How you landed the interview is now beside the point. How well you conduct yourself in it, on the other hand, is everything.

> **job interview:** an interview, a formal meeting or a conversation, designed to determine whether an applicant is suitable for a position of employment.

For all the nervousness and uncertainty interviews can cause, there is nothing mysterious about them. Your **suitability for the job**, as the above definition mentions, is at the heart of the matter.

The job interview is simply a "getting to know you" conversation that you have with an employer before either of you make any commitments. Compare it to a first date, an audition for a play, or a game of extreme ping-pong. You can experience an interview in a number of ways.

- You and the employer may be in a room, sitting across from each other.
- You may face a panel of employees, each of them throwing out questions for you to answer.
- You and several other applicants may be together, each of you fighting and clawing your way to distinction from the pack in your efforts to impress the interviewer.

- Job interviews can occur in person, over the telephone, or online. Most are designed to screen a field of candidates down to a select few.
- You may go to only one job interview before a hiring decision is made, or you may go to several for the same job.
- Some job interviews are designed to see how you behave, handle stress, or navigate social situations in fictitious workplace scenarios.
- You may be asked to make a formal presentation.

No two interviews are exactly alike. There are, however, consistencies you can usually count on. During the course of an interview this is what typically happens:

Stage 1: Introductions are made while everyone shakes hands and sits down. The interviewer initiates small talk, designed to break the ice. This stage lasts a few minutes.

Stage 2: The interviewer begins by discussing the job and the company. He asks questions based on the resume you gave him. The length of time spent in this stage varies depending on how interested the employer is in your qualifications and whether other candidates are waiting to be interviewed after you. If this part of the interview lasts at least 15 minutes, that usually indicates employer interest.

Stage 3: The employer then asks you if you have any questions. This is your opportunity to respond with good questions that hopefully will impress him or her.

Stage 4: The interview winds down. You ask (if the interviewer hasn't already brought this up) when you may expect to hear their decision, and whether you may call by such and such time to follow up. You thank the employer for the interview as you once again shake hands and officially end the interview.

Stage 5: You finally breathe, relieved to have the ordeal behind you.

Each organization has its own way of interviewing prospective employees. Some employers stick to a specific script of questions, never deviating from it. Others may improvise more just to see where the conversation goes, perhaps asking more probing questions.

Employer personalities can play a big role in the direction of the interview. The person conducting the interview may be good at it, keeping the discussion focused and flowing. Or he might be a lousy interviewer. Whatever set of circumstances you find yourself in, you'll have to adapt as you go along. Doing that will be easier if you understand what employers want from you in the first place.

What Employers Really Want From You

It's simple if you think about it. Employers, for the most part, want to know three basic things about you.

1. Can you do the job?   Do you have the requisite skills to do the job? Have you done a similar type of job before? If the position requires a current license or certification, do you have it?

2. Will you do the job? You may be qualified for the job, but will you actually do it? Do you appear interested in it? What's your motivation?

3. Will you fit in? Will you get along with other employees? The most qualified employee isn't worth hiring if he's going to be difficult to manage and disruptive to the organization.

You want your next job interview to be a successful one that results in an offer of employment. To get that job offer, you must answer these three questions for the employer regardless of whether she actually asks them.

Before the Interview

1. Research and learn as much as you can about the employer.

You already know something about your would-be employer. You did manage to wrangle a job interview. Do you know enough, though? It would be easy to show up and answer the generic questions such as:

- What do you know about our company?
- Why do you want to work here?
- What do you think this job involves?
- How can you make a difference here, based on what you already know?

You have to know the answers to these basic questions before you show up for the interview, so that you can then move on to a more meaningful conversation about what you can do for the company.

Anyone can answer the easy questions. You don't want to be just anyone, though. You want to be **the one** they have been looking for in the recruitment process. To be **the one**, you have to demonstrate that you are not just any candidate.

Accordingly, in addition to the above questions that an employer might ask you about the company, here are sample questions that you should research ahead of time:

- Where is the company headed? What is their mission or vision for the future?
- Are there advancement opportunities with this company?
- How does the company seem to treat its employees?
- What is the corporate culture or the personality of the company?
- Are competitive salaries offered? Comprehensive benefits?
- What is the general state of the industry in which this company operates?
- Would you be able to continue employment with the company through a PCS move?

To start your research, go to the organization's website, where you can see how they present themselves to the public. As you examine the site, keep in mind that the company wants to show itself in the most favorable light possible.

Try to really get to know the company by searching online beyond their website. What do publically posted financial reports suggest about the company? Do they project growth, diversification, or are they strictly niche focused? Is the company portrayed negatively or positively in the news? Is it a military-friendly company?

Examples of websites that may provide you with good information on companies you are targeting, either free or for a fee, include:

Careerleak	www.careerleak.com
D&B's Million Dollar Database	www.dnbmdd.com
Glassdoor	www.glassdoor.com
Hoovers (a D&B company)	www.hooversonline.com
Military Spouse Employment Partnership	www.msepjobs.com
Moody's	www.moodys.com
New York Times	www.nytimes.com
Standard and Poor's	www.standardandpoors.com
Thomas Net	www.thomasnet.com
Vault	www.vault.com

Wall Street Journal   www.wsj.com
Wetfeet   www.wetfeet.com

You can also check the best/worst employers lists compiled by various magazines and organizations. Here are sites that usually post them annually:

- CNN Money's 100 Best Companies to Work For
  www.cnn.com
- Military Spouse Magazine
  Top 10 Military Spouse Friendly Employers
  www.milspouse.com
- Working Mother 100 Best Companies
  www.workingmother.com
- GI Jobs Top 100 Military Friendly Employers
  www.gijobs.com
- Civilian Jobs Most Valuable Employers (MVE) for Military®
  www.civilianjobs.com
- Washington Technology Top 100 Government Contractors
  www.washingtontechnology.com

Don't forget to talk to any friendly contacts you have at the company and try to get their take on the company. A visit the local Chamber of Commerce or Better Business Bureau might also be worth your while.

Other sources of information to consider: local businesspersons, ministers or pastors, physicians/dentists, beauticians, teachers – in short, anyone you come into contact with might be able to share interesting information with you.

Research the company in several different ways to piece together a clear picture of who they are, what they do, and how you might fit in with them.

2. Decide what you will wear to the interview.

First impressions count whether you like it or not. You may be the perfect person for the job, but if the first impression you create distresses more than impresses, the employer may not bother to find out.

To create the best impression possible, take the time to plan what you will wear to the interview and how you "carry" yourself.

It's your image, baby. Work it.

There are two classic rules to keep in mind when it comes to selecting clothing for an interview.

> **Rule #1:** Dress appropriately for the job and the industry for which you are interviewing.

> **Rule #2:** Dress up rather than down.

Does this mean you need to go out and buy a whole new wardrobe? No, it does not.

On the other hand, if you want an excuse to indulge in some good old-fashioned retail therapy, go for it. Otherwise, take a closer look at what is inside your closet and you will probably be able to put something suitable (pun intended) together.

Here are some more detailed thoughts on the subject:

Smart Choice Outfit:

- You can never go wrong with a decent quality two-piece matched business suit that fits well. Even if you wouldn't wear it every day to the job if you were hired, go with the suit. It communicates a professional image, which is what you are striving for here.

- If you want to buy a new one, live on the edge and invest in the best quality you can afford, opting for wool, wool blends, or good quality natural and synthetic fibers. Keep the fabric of the suit to a solid color or small weave pattern.

- Women should choose conservative colors, such as navy, dark gray, or black for their suit, and wear a coordinated color blouse if the suit calls for it. Suits, in this case, can be a jacket and skirt or a jacket and tailored pants. The skirt length should be at your knees when you're standing up.

- The same advice holds true for men minus the black suit because black tends to look too formal for the occasion. With the suit, wear a long-sleeve white, light blue, or conservative-striped shirt and a nice tie that isn't red.

- Red worn by anyone in an interview creates an unspoken statement of power and dominance. You can be the big dog after you're hired. Get hired first.

- Take good care of your suit and it will take good care of you for many years. Simple practices like hanging it up after you take it off and occasionally dry cleaning it go a long way to making your suit last.

Smart Choice Accessories:

- Avoid jewelry overkill, opting for simple and classic in your choice of watch, earrings, necklace, and rings. A good rule of thumb to follow is that if people can hear or smell you coming or going, leave it off.

- Your shoes should be clean, in good condition, comfortable, and professional looking. Nothing tanks a great interview outfit like a old pair of shoes. Or the wrong pair of socks or stockings with the right pair of shoes. Or sandals. And do not ever expose your naked toes. Women can't go wrong with close-toed pumps. Save the stilettos for the party after you've landed the job. Men, particularly former servicemembers turned spouses, should not wear the military-style black patent shoes.

- Body piercings, for better or worse, can be distracting. If you have them, consider leaving them at home. You want the employer's attention on your skills, not on your tongue unless of course the interviewer has one too. You may want to consider covering up body art, which can also be distracting.

- Take a pen and paper to make notes. Bring extra copies of your resume. The employer may not have yours available, or there may be other people in the room who would like to look at it. Carry all of these things in an attractive portfolio or briefcase that you have cleaned out ahead of time.

Additional Tips:

- If you're wearing pantyhose, carry an extra pair in your purse in case of any last-minute runs that can be corrected before going into the interview itself.

- If you carry a purse, it should be small so you don't end up juggling a briefcase and/or portfolio as well as a purse. Bonus points for you if your shoes and purse match.

- It may go without saying, but wear deodorant and little if any perfume or cologne. If you smoke, you should stop. People care about you. If you smoke before a job interview, you will stink and no one will be impressed. See, no smoking is win-win for everyone. Also, companies are increasingly requiring that employees be non-smokers.

- And of course, rules of good grooming win out. Your hair, facial or otherwise, should be clean and brushed. Fingernails should be dirt-free, trimmed or nicely manicured.

Beyond the Obvious: How You Carry Yourself

Yes, looks matter. How you conduct yourself matters, too. Taken together, appearance and conduct comprise the whole package that is you, visible to the interviewer. You can communicate a positive self-image by the following:

- Maintain good posture and eye contact. Avoid crossing your arms and legs in a way that keeps others at a distance.

- Think positive thoughts. Be confident but not arrogant. It's said that the body goes where the mind leads it.

- Don't calm interview jitters by tapping your fingers, jiggling a leg, or chewing gum. It will only make you look nervous and be annoying to those around you.

- Breathe normally and keep yourself focused.

3. Anticipate and prepare for interview questions.

You want to feel comfortable in the job interview, able to readily and fully answer the questions you are asked. Before the interview, consider what questions might come up and draft, mentally at least, a basic answer. Don't memorize answers to recite to the employer later. You don't want to sound like a recording, but you do want to answer questions completely, putting yourself in the best light possible.

As you prep your thoughts, keep in mind the following:

- Focus your answers on the positive only. Answer the questions in a manner that highlights your strengths and capabilities.

- Be sure to fully answer the questions. Providing one-word answers won't help you. Give the employer a **real** sense of what you can do, have done, and how effectively you can communicate it. You're the real deal. Don't shortchange yourself.

- Practice active listening, avoiding the mistake of making assumptions. The first few words pour out of the interviewer's mouth and you know what else is coming. Right? Maybe, maybe not. Don't mentally start answering the question **before** you've heard it completely. You don't want to give an inappropriate answer, which won't help your cause.

- Be honest in your answers but don't provide gory damaging details if they exist.

- **Never,** ever make negative comments about past employers or co-workers during a job interview. Even if you were the innocent party in the whole debacle, you don't want to come across as bitter and negative yourself.

Here are some of the more commonly asked questions and strategies for answering them:

"Tell me about yourself."

You can answer this one in many different ways depending on who is asking it. In this case, an employer is asking, so keep your answer focused on the professional you and not on your personal life. An employer doesn't really want to know that you were an only child, grew up on a farm, and graduated with honors from high school. She wants to know who you are on a professional level.

"What do you know about our company?"

Provide an insightful "big picture" answer to this question, showing that you've done your homework. The employer will be impressed and won't have to waste precious time bringing you up to speed on the basics.

"What do you know about our competitors?"

At a minimum, be able to identify the top two or three. Bonus points for you if you comment intelligently on how the company you're interviewing with does things better than the competition.

"What matters the most to you in your job?"

It may be all about the money to you, but you'll impress an employer more if you cite other aspects of your job.

"Why do you want to work here?"

Have a solid and thoughtful reply for a question like this. Your prior research on the company or organization, coupled with your own personal reasons for applying the job, will help you to answer this one in a positive way.

"Why did you leave your last job?"

This could be a difficult question to answer. If you say you left your last job because of a PCS move, you immediately make the employer think it will happen again. Instead, focus on some other, also truthful, reason if possible. If you left your last job under less than ideal circumstances (such as being fired or laid off), be truthful. It's the right thing to do. Besides, employers often call previous employers to verify employment periods or to get obtain references. Keep your explanation brief and focus instead on the positive that has come out of it.

"What is your greatest strength/weakness?"

Everyone has strengths and weakness. The key to answering questions about them in a job interview is to express each in a positive light. Strengths are easy to address and always make you look good. Weaknesses, on the other hand, have to be handled with more care. For example, if one of your weaknesses is never being on time, don't brag about it. Don't even bring it up. Instead, say that you have a hard time leaving the office at the end of the day when you are in the middle of a project.

"Tell me about a time when you..."

Employers want to know more about you than what they see on the resume. They want to get a genuine sense of how you handle situations. To understand that, they may ask you questions like *"Tell me about a time when you failed on the job"* or *"Tell me about a time when you had to work with a difficult colleague."* This type of question is based on the theory that past behavior predicts future behavior.

"What is your greatest accomplishment/failure?"

The same theory applies here. How you answer this one gives an employer an insight into what matters the most on the job to you (your accomplishment) and how you handle the situation when things go wrong. If you are asked the failure side to this question, be sure you reveal the lesson you learned that will help you in the future. Keep your response positive at all times.

"What did you like most about your last job?"

Here the employer is trying to visualize the fit between you and the job you're interviewing for based on how you related to your last job. For example, if your favorite task in your past job was working with customers directly and the job you are now trying to get hired for would involve high customer involvement, that's a potential fit and would work in your favor.

"Why should I hire you?"

This can be an intimidating question, to be sure. Be ready for it. Bold questions require bold answers. A short sweet answer might be:

> *You should hire me because I'm the best candidate for the job and you won't be sorry.*

You could also answer the question with a supported case:

> *You need someone to do x, y, and z. I have five years experience doing that and can bring that new perspective that you're looking for in an employee to this company.*

"How do you spend your spare time?"

Be careful answering this one. It could work for or against you. Remember, employers want to know if you can do the job, if you will do the job, and if you will fit in. The answer you provide to this question may help them determine whether you will fit in with others in the company or not. Avoid mentioning any controversial hobbies or activities you might participate in.

"What qualifies you for this job?"

Focus your answer on the specific skills needed to do the job. Review the job announcement in addition to your resume **before** the interview to refresh your memory in case you are asked this one.

"What would your last employer say about you?"

Before you leave your current employer, ask to use his name as reference and ask him what he would say about you if a potential new employer asked him about you. If you didn't do this already, then wing it. If your relationship with your former employer was a good one, this should be an easy one to answer, keeping your response accomplishment-based.

"What's your five-year plan?"

Most employers like to hire people who have an idea of what they want to do in their lives. Your own five-year plan may involve a soldier, a sailboat, and a pitcher of margaritas, but that's not the one the employer wants to hear about. A vague but acceptable answer might go something like this:

> *No one can predict the future, of course, but I like to think that the next five years will show a progression in my career. Hopefully, will happen for me here at this company where we can benefit each other. I also plan to begin a master's degree program soon and I anticipate that it will open other doors for me, perhaps here, in the future.*

"How would you make yourself valuable to this company?"

Answer this question by first thinking about what is most important to the company. Is it customer satisfaction? Sales volume? Meeting deadlines? How you can add to things that are most important to the company? What skills and/or talents do you have that will help them achieve their goals? That's what you focus on here.

"Do you work better alone or with others?"

You can't go wrong here saying that you work well in either situation. If, however, you know the job is one where you will be by yourself for days at a time and you're good at that, say so. It directly supports the job at hand.

4. Be prepared for illegal questions you may be asked

Knowingly or not, employers sometimes ask you illegal questions about your race, color, sex, religion, citizenship, birthplace, disabilities, and marital and family status.

Examples of such questions include:

How old are you?
Are you married?
Who do you live with?
Are you pregnant or planning to be?
How many children do you have?
Do you have child care arrangements in place?
Do you have a disability?
Have you ever been arrested?
How much do you weigh?
Have you had any recent illnesses or operations?
Is your husband/wife/partner in the military?
What holidays do you celebrate?
What does your spouse think about your career?
Tell me about your family.
What religion do you practice?
Do you smoke or drink?
How far away do you live?

There are a couple different strategies to help you address these questions. How you choose to answer them depends on you and your level of comfort on the subject.

Take a look at this example of an illegal question and the different ways you could choose to answer it.

There is always an expressed intent behind each interview question, illegal or not. If you can identify that intent and answer it, employers should be satisfied with your answer.

If any question truly offends you, you have the choice to end the interview by simply leaving. Chances are good you won't get offered the job, but under the circumstances you probably wouldn't want it anyhow.

ILLEGAL QUESTION:
Is your husband/wife/partner in the military?

You can refuse to answer the question: I don't think that is relevant to our interview and I'd rather not answer.

You can answer the question breifly and move on: Yes, he is.

You can ask for clarification on the point: That's an interesting question. I'm not sure I understand why it matters. Could you explain how it relates to the job in question so I understand better?

You can answer the intent of the question: We are new to the community and hope to make it home for many years to come.

---

5. Know how to handle salary questions

Typically, questions about salary don't occur in the first interview. They usually come up in the second or third interview when the field of potential candidates has been whittled down to a select few. If you are asked this question during your first interview, turn it back on the employer: *What salary are you prepared to offer?*

If the ball gets tossed back in your court to answer, then you can either say that you want to learn more about what the job involves before discussing it or you can provide a **salary range** to the employer. If you provide a salary range, make sure it is one that you have researched appropriately and overstate it by 10-15%.

If you are already working, you probably have a good idea of your salary requirements. If you are new to a community, you might want to check your expectations against the geographical realities, however. For example, some jobs pay more in Washington, DC than they do in the Greater Fort Leonard Wood, Missouri area.

There are many ways to research salary data. Here are a few websites:

Salary.com:	www.salary.com
Payscale:	www.payscale.com
CBSalary:	www.cbsalary.com
Bureau of Labor Statistics:	www.bls.gov
Vault Salary Reports:	www.vault.com

You can sometimes get an idea of salaries paid by companies by checking out their job announcements or by talking to others who work there. Be careful about the latter, however. The subject of salaries can be taboo depending on the industry, company, and job.

Some other points to keep in mind regarding salary negotiation:

- **Never** be the first one to bring up the topic of compensation or benefits. Let the employer do it.
- Employers will generally not bring up the topic of compensation unless they are seriously considering you for the job. Keep in mind, when the time does come, that benefits can be negotiated as well.
- Negotiate salary and benefits separately, being able to fully explain why your skills are worth it.
- Keep the negotiation conversation a positive one, offering potential win-win solutions.
- Get any offers of employment in writing before accepting a job.

6. Think of questions you may want to ask the employer

What goes around, comes around. It's true for questions too. In the job interview, not only do you get to answer a laundry list of them, you have the opportunity to ask a few of them yourself as well.

Think about those questions before you go to the interview, too. Make a short list of questions and take it with you. During the course of the conversation, your questions might get answered before you have an opportunity to ask them. That's all right. The point is to get the information in the first place so you can make an educated decision about the job if you receive an offer.

Likewise, new questions might come to you during the interview itself. That's a good thing. It means you're thinking about more than just the face value of the conversation.

Here are a few questions to consider asking:

What do you see as the most important focus for the first 90 days on this job?

How do employees work together at this company?

In your opinion, what are the greatest challenges facing this company?

What qualities matter the most in the ideal person for this job?

Are there advancement opportunities here? How so?

Is creativity encouraged? Are new ideas for doing business welcome?

On the Day of the Interview

Plan to arrive about 10 minutes early to the interview. Be nice to everyone whom you see when you walk in the door. You can't be 100% sure who holds influence within the organization.

Curb interview-day jitters by focusing on clear speech – yours, that is.

- Avoid using killer fillers such as *you know, like*, and *um*. One hiring manager confided to me that she starts to count how many times she hears these speech patterns instead of listening to what is important.

- Speak the same language. Remember when you were a newbie military spouse and felt like you had been dropped down in the middle of a foreign land, left to figure out the meanings of acronyms such as LES, a PX/BX, ACUs, and TDY? Same principle applies here. Every job location, position, or group has its own acronym language, but outsiders don't always know it. If you use acronyms, make sure that the hiring manager or the job screener understands what you are saying.

If you are offered something to drink or eat, politely decline lest you end up with crumbs on your face, literally and otherwise.

Do your best to **appear relaxed**, using body language that suggests you are interested and present in the moment.

If it helps you to **remember details** later, take notes but don't make a big production of it.

Listen closely. Don't try to analyze what you hear now. Soak it all in now, making sure you understand what is being said. There will be plenty of time to analyze it in more depth after the interview.

Determine the next step in the hiring process before you leave the interview.

Thank the employer for the interview. If you are offered a job on the spot, express your appreciation and tell her that you will seriously consider it.

After the Interview

The interview is over and you are relieved. Hopefully, you came away from it far more knowledgeable than you were before you went to it. The face-time portion of the process may be over for the moment, but there is still work to be done.

You'll want to analyze the information you learned and evaluate whether or not you are still interested in the job or the company as a result.

Shortly afterwards, within 24 hours, send a thank-you note either in hand-written or email form. This not only gives you the opportunity to express your thanks again, but also the chance to remind the employer of your interest and specific skills.

If you haven't heard back from the employer in a week or so, call him to touch base and see where he is in the recruitment process.

Don't assume you will be offered the job because you interviewed well. Other could have interviewed well, too.

Don't stop looking for other jobs. Something even better might be right around the corner.

INTERVIEW CHECKLIST

Before the Interview

❑ Research the company and the job position in detail.

❑ Select your interview outfit and coordinating accessories.

❑ Rehearse answers to common interview questions.

❑ Compile a list of questions to ask the employer.

❑ Know where the interview is scheduled to take place and how to get there.

❑ Get a good night's rest before the day of the interview.

On the Day of the Interview

❑ Eat breakfast/brunch/lunch before the interview.

❑ Check traffic reports before heading out. You may need to leave earlier.

❑ Turn off your cell phone before you arrive at the interview.

❑ Show up 10-15 minutes before the scheduled appointment.

❑ Offer a firm handshake when greeting the employer.

❑ Maintain good eye contact and avoid negative body language.

❑ Appear confident and poised. Show enthusiasm.

❑ Answer questions completely and thoughtfully.

❑ Make sure you are actively listening. Take notes if necessary.

❑ Speak clearly and in a way the employer will be able to understand.

❑ Determine the next step in the hiring process before leaving the interview.

❑ Thank the employer verbally for the interview.

After the Interview

❑ Conduct a post-interview analysis.

❑ Send a thank-you note to the employer(s).

❑ Follow up on the interview within 1-2 weeks.

❑ Continue your job search efforts.

PART III
Smart Job Solutions for a
Military Lifestyle

9

Ask Janet: Tough Questions and Real Answers

NO MATTER HOW many times you go through the job search process, some new tough challenge always seems to present itself. Or maybe it's not a new challenge, but one that you may handle differently because you are now older and wiser… or not.

Throughout my career working with military spouses on a wide variety of employment-related issues, I have been asked many tough questions. In this chapter, I am sharing with you some of those questions and my suggested answers to them. The questions, as you will see, cover all kinds of topics from practicality to policy and everything in between. Nothing is off limits.

As you read over them, you may find the answers you need, ready to apply in your situation without any additional thought or researching.

On the other hand, the answers may cause you to think of even more questions. While that may seem counter-productive, it's not. It's a good sign that you are carefully analyzing the finer points of the issue under question, so that you can come to the best conclusion for yourself, given your unique perspective on the situation.

Finally, if you don't see your question here, email it to me at janetfarley@janetfarley.com and I'll do my best to find the answer to it.

Federal Employment

1. *I have been trying to get a federal job on our base for the last year and a half without any luck. I see other spouses transfer in and get hired right away. What am I doing wrong?*

It can drive you mad, can't it? Sometimes there doesn't seem to be any rhyme or reason as to who gets selected and who doesn't. There are a number of actions you may consider taking in this case:

1. **Talk to those other spouses** who are getting hired. Ask them how they've managed to do it. Whatever they did worked and what you're doing isn't. The truth may hurt, but you need to compare your strategy with theirs and figure out a better one for yourself.

2. **Improve your networking activities.** By talking to the spouses who have been hired, you are doing that. Talk with anyone whose path you cross; they might know influential people who can help you attain your goal. Create or re-ignite other professional relationships as well, particularly with those in the areas where you want to work. Join professional organizations in your location or online.

3. **Revise your federal resume.** If you need help, visit the employment readiness program at the family center or call on Military One Source's Spouse Career Center for assistance. You may not be targeting your resume as effectively as possible. You can also pay a professional resume writer to re-write it for you, but it will be expensive. Books that can help you include *The Book of U.S. Government Jobs* and *Federal Resume Guidebook* (see Career Resources on pages 176-177).

4. **Consider applying for different jobs** within the federal system that may better match your skills and abilities or apply outside of it altogether. You can always continue to strive towards landing a federal job while you are drawing a civilian paycheck.

5. **Do volunteer work in the meantime.** It's a win-win-win. You get to keep your skills from getting rusty. You get to network for a paying job more vigorously. The organization or community where you volunteer benefits from your expert assistance and dedication.

6. **Don't give up.** Patience and persistence can be painful but they work.

2. *I don't understand the Military Spouse Preference. Isn't it supposed to guarantee me a job?*

The Military Spouse Preference does not guarantee you a job because you are a military spouse. You can read more about it in Chapter 5, on pages 76-77.

3. *I am not a U.S. citizen but am married to a military servicemember. Why is it so hard to get a federal job?*

According to USAJobs, only U.S. citizens and nationals may be appointed in the competitive civil service. Federal agencies, may, however, hire certain non-citizens who meet specific requirements in the excepted service (see http://www.makingthedifference.org/federaljobs/excepted-service.shtml) or in the Senior Executive Service (see http://www.opm.gov/fedcdp/). Since you are not a U.S. citizen, you may need to change your employment goals for the moment at least. For more details, refer to USAJobs online at:http://www.usajobs.gov/ResourceCenter/Index/Interactive/NonCitizensEmployment#icc.

4. *There is a federal job I am interested in applying for, but I don't fall into the category of eligible applicants. Shouldn't I just apply and see what happens? Maybe they will be blinded by my awesome qualifications and hire me anyway, right?*

Don't waste your time applying for jobs for which you are ineligible. You may be well qualified for a job, but if you are not eligible to apply for it in the first place, your resume won't make the cut no matter how good it may be.

5. *How can I tell if I'm eligible to apply for a federal job?*

Read the job vacancy announcement. It will tell you everything you ever wanted to know but were afraid to ask.

Job Search

6. *How do I find out what jobs are available in my local community?*

There are many ways to find out what jobs are open. At the risk of repeating Chapter 3 here, suffice it to say that you have to key yourself into the employment possibilities within a given community. You have to know where you can go to obtain assistance in getting a job. You have to be willing to adjust your expectations if the conditions aren't there to support your current ones. To fully answer your question, see Chapter 3.

7. *What are the fastest growing jobs?*

Good question. If you were to ask any of the nearly 10% currently unemployed in America, they may tell you that there are none. That wouldn't be true, however.

According to Career OneStop (www.careeronestop.org), a U.S. Department of Labor site, these are the top five fastest growing occupations requiring post-secondary training or an associate degree:

#1 Skin care specialists
#2 Dental hygienists
#3 Veterinary technologists and technicians
#4 Physical therapist assistants
#5 Environmental engineering technicians

Here are the top five for those requiring a bachelor's degree or higher:

#1 Biomedical engineers
#2 Financial examiners
#3 Medical scientists (but not epidemiologists)
#4 Physician assistants
#5 Biochemists and biophysicists

And last but not least, here are the top five requiring only work experience or on-the-job training:

#1 Home health aides
#2 Personal and home care aides
#3 Physical therapist aides
#4 Dental assistants
#5 Medical assistants

8. Should I make up my own "business" card for job search purposes?

When you are in the business of looking for a job and doing a lot of networking, having a basic business card with your name, contact information, and area of specialty noted on it is a good idea. It's not exactly a resume, but it may lead to the opportunity to provide one and it's a lot easier to hand your card to someone you just met instead of your resume.

If you opt to use a business card, be sure the card presents a professional image rather than a "social" image. Splurge on good card stock and avoid the freebie cards offered by some companies. Those freebies usually contain advertising about the company providing them on the reverse side of the card, which will take attention away from advertising about **you**.

Keep the card uncluttered and easy to read. At a minimum, it should contain your name, your address, telephone number, and email address.

If you have a website, a professionally written blog, or you tweet about your career in a way that you don't mind potential employers knowing about, you could include that contact information on your card.

9. How can my volunteer work experience help me land a paying job?

Your volunteer work experience can be instrumental in finding a paying job. If you can't get the paid experience you need to build a career or work in a given area, then you volunteer to do it. After you have racked up what can be called experience in that area, you put that information on your resume and thereby increase your chances of landing a paying job in that area. You are no longer someone who only wants to work in specific area; you are now someone who has relevant work experience in that area. It doesn't matter whether you earned a paycheck while gaining that experience or not.

10. What is the most effective job search technique?

Networking. See Chapter Three for more details to help you network your way into a better job.

11. What is the least effective job search technique?

You won't get results by mass mailing or emailing your resume to employers. Or by posting your resume to big online job boards and then just sitting back and waiting for someone to contact you with a job offer. You have to **focus** your job search efforts for the best chance of getting hired.

12. I hate talking about my accomplishments to employers. It feels like I'm bragging and that just seems wrong.

Not to sound harsh, but get over it. It may help you to stop thinking about it as bragging.

Bragging is boasting about something in an arrogant way. Talking about your accomplishments shouldn't fall into that category. When you talk with an employer about the good work you have done in the past, you are trying to show that you are competent, qualified, and able to do similar good things for his or her company. You communicate these facts of life in a professional manner, without arrogance, and you propel forward your effort to get hired.

13. There are no job opportunities in my community. Really.

In a word, that sucks. It happens though. When it does, you have some deep thinking to do on the matter. You need to consider what you can do that can carry you forward either until jobs materialize or you move out of there.

Some ideas to help you jumpstart that process:

- Create your own job, set up an internship, or start your own business.
- Focus on enhancing your future marketability by taking courses.
- Volunteer in an area where a job could potentially open up.

14. I am absolutely sick of my current job and want to look for a new one. Am I obligated to tell my current employer what I'm doing?

No, you are not obligated to tell your current employer. In fact, you shouldn't share that information at this point anyway.

If you can't stand your job and want a new one, discreetly begin a job search during your lunch hour or when you are at home.

Once you have accepted a new job, then you can tell your employer that you're outta there. Do your best to give at least a two-week notice, to enable your employer to find a replacement.

Go out as gracefully as you came in. First impressions and last impressions will follow you throughout your professional life.

15. We are expecting orders any day now and I will have to give my manager notice that I'm leaving. We don't know for sure when we are leaving, but I need to keep the job as long as possible. How do I handle this?

By keeping quiet for now. You don't have exact dates yet and until you do, don't screw yourself out of a job. Things could always change and you could end up staying in place longer than you previously thought. Once you have definite dates marked on the calendar, have a chat with your employer, giving as much notice as possible.

16. I found a job but I'm way overqualified for it. Should I take it?

Maybe and maybe not. The real question here should be, do you want to do the job?

You might be overqualified but if it is something that matters to you and you have a burning desire to do it, go for it. Passion can't be corralled by qualifications.

On the other hand, if you are settling for the job because you can't find one that does fit your qualifications, think twice before accepting it. When you settle in, you may become restless and dissatisfied. You end up being no fun to be around when you feel your talents aren't being appropriately applied or appreciated.

If you want to take the job because you need the paycheck, go ahead. You can discreetly continue your job search at the same time.

17. I have a plan to get a job. What if it doesn't work and I can't find a good job after all?

If Plan A fails, go to Plan B. If Plan B tanks, go to Plan C.

Plan A may be to find a specific job. If you haven't been able to land that job, shift your efforts to Plan B, which might be to land the next best job in your mind. If that doesn't work either, maybe Plan C means you register to work on a temporary basis somewhere until your Plan A or B happens for you.

Have a plan. Have a back-up plan. Have a back-up plan to your back-up plan.

Federal Support

18. What is MSEP and just how is it supposed to help me?

Once upon a time there was the Army Spouse Employment Partnership and it was good. It brought together military-friendly employers with military spouses. The program has since been expanded into the Military Spouse Employment Partnership (MSEP), which does the same thing, only for all military spouses. If you haven't accessed it online yet, do it now at www. msepjobs.militaryonesource.mil. You can get free resume writing and job search assistance, and you can search their database for jobs.

19. What is Joining Forces all about?

According to the official site, Joining Forces is a national initiative launched by First Lady Michelle Obama and Dr. Jill Biden to encourage everyone to "join forces" and support our military servicemembers and their families. You can learn about it and how to get involved at www.whitehouse.gov/joiningforces. One of the most positive outcomes to date regarding spouse employment is the MSEP mentioned above. Kudos to the current First and Second Ladies for elevating the awareness of military spouse employment issues and for encouraging workable solutions. Stay tuned and I predict we'll see even more good things come out of this initiative.

20. My spouse is a U.S. Army major and I am not eligible for the MyCAA program because of his rank. Are there similar education-funding assistance programs for spouses who have been around for a while and who plan on staying in the military? It doesn't seem fair.

You're not alone in your thinking. Unfortunately, funding is tight and will get tighter long before it gets better again. MyCAA was a good idea, but it doesn't have an adequate budget. Don't expect it to open up to longer-serving families anytime soon.

For now, there are three words: scholarships, grants, and loans. See Chapter Two, page 17, for information on them.

Licensure and Certification

21. My job requires a state certification and/or license. If we move, do my credentials move with me?

It depends on your job and the state requirements at your next duty station.

22. What sources of funding are available to military spouses seeking certification in a career field?

If you meet the eligibility requirements, you may be able to take advantage of up to $4,000 through the MyCAA, a career development and employment assistance program sponsored by the DoD. Other scholarships, grants, and loans may be available to you as well. See Chapter Two for more information.

23. I became a registered nurse thinking it was a job that would PCS with me anywhere. State licensing and certification requirements are making that difficult. Did I make a career mistake?

It can probably feel like you did when you find yourself having to shell out bucks every PCS move just to be able to work in that location for a couple of years.

It wasn't a mistake if you love nursing. If you only chose the field because you thought it was something you could do easily from place to place, then maybe you did make a mistake. Let me elaborate.

Thirty-three percent of professional military spouses work in career fields that require licenses, such as nursing and other medically related occupations. Other career fields also often require licensure; for example, teaching, social work, cosmetology, occupational therapy, massage therapy, and even fortunetelling.

In theory, portable jobs are good because they can PCS with us. In reality, they can be problematic because of the different requirements for state licensure and certification. You might be able to work in Virginia where you are currently stationed, but not in California where you are getting ready to PCS. You might have to re-certify all over again and that can cost you out-of-pocket bucks and time away from your profession.

Some states have reciprocity in the matter and allow you to practice your profession from place to place without having to become re-certified or obtain a new license. Or, in some cases, the requirements may be altered and abbreviated. There isn't a nationally recognized one-size-fits-all credential, however.

At the upper policy levels of DoD where they really do try to make things better for all military spouses, they realize this and are working toward solutions to this problem. Truly committed individuals within the State Liaison and Educational Opportunity office, an office of the Military Community and Family Policy, are working on your behalf with the states to eliminate these kinds of barriers.

As of now (as this book goes to press), they have succeeded in getting 16 states to adopt laws or close to adopting them so that military spouses may continue their careers more easily from state to state.

Military spouses who choose to work in a profession that requires licensure or certification have to accept the reality that the individual state requirements are not going to go away. States have an obligation to protect their citizens, and one way they do that is by requiring all individuals in the state who work in certain professions to meet certain standards.

If you want to make your job and your military lifestyle more compatible, you can do the following:

- Research state requirements before you move there, and get the process started in advance.
- If you are eligible, use the funding provided by MyCAA to help you get what you need, up to the $4,000 ceiling.
- Contact your state representative and express your concerns and offer suggestions for making the matter better for everyone.
- If you find yourself stuck in limbo waiting on paperwork to come through, work in a fringe job (a job around your usual job) in the interim to maintain your network and to keep your other skills current.

Self-Employment

24. *I want to work from home because I have small children and can't afford daycare. Besides, they are only young once and I don't want to miss anything. I read about a work-at-home opportunity in our local newspaper, and it said all I had to do was send $29.95 to an address and they would send me information about it. Should I do it?*

No, you should **not** do it. **Never** pay someone else for the opportunity to work from home. That is a scam.

Are you sure you can't afford daycare? Check with the Child Development Center on the nearest military installation. Believe it or not, the rates there are often more reasonable than civilian rates, depending upon your family's income (i.e., your spouse's rank).

In-home childcare offered by others may be an option as well.

The National Association of Child Care Resources and Referral Agencies (www.naccrra.org), which partners with the military services, can also assist you in locating affordable childcare.

There are many ways you can work from home, including offering your own daycare services. Start to explore some of the home-based business options that might match your skills and interests. Once you've narrowed down your thoughts on it, prepare a business plan and go for it.

Take a look at the Go-To Resources for Self-Employment on pages 164-171 to get started on the process.

25. *Is it possible to set up a contract to provide services on call through Morale Welfare and Recreation (MWR)?*

It depends on the community and what is needed. You can do this in many places, however. Contact the MWR office on the nearest installation for details regarding local opportunities.

Unemployment Benefits

26. We have to move again. Am I eligible for unemployment benefits?

It depends. Thirty-eight states currently provide eligibility for unemployment compensation to military spouses who leave employment because of a military move.

To find out whether you can receive unemployment benefits, contact the state Department of Labor in the state where you currently work. To access the State Unemployment Insurance Benefits page, go to the following link: http://workforcesecurity.doleta.gov/unemploy/uifactsheet.asp.

Discrimination

27. Employers seem really interested in me until they learn that I am a military spouse and may have to move in a couple years. How can I convince them to give me a chance?

Don't you hate that? I do.

First, focus your job search efforts on employers that understand and appreciate the military to begin with. You can find out about some of those employers through the Military Spouse Employment Partnership (www.mspejobs.militaryonesource.mil).

Second, in an interview, keep the emphasis on the job and what you can do to excel in it. You don't need to offer up private details of your life. Employers shouldn't ask. If they do and you oblige with an answer, don't emphasize that you might eventually move.

The truth of the matter is you just don't know how long you will end up living somewhere. A two-year tour can always turn into a four-year or longer one. It happens all the time.

An employer worth working for in the first place will focus on **you** and what you can do rather than on whom you are married to and how long you may be around.

The Big Picture

28. *Over the many PCS moves and our years in the military, I feel like my career has suffered. I'm not even sure you can call it a career because it is really just a string of jobs, loosely related at times, that I managed to land along the way. Should I be looking for just another job?*

You know, I think we all just do the best we can under the circumstances, whether we are living a mobile military lifestyle or a planted in one place as a civilian. Sometimes the right opportunities come along and we take advantage of them. Sometimes they don't and we deal with it. We make choices along the way, whether they are the choices we want to make or not. In the end, we live with the outcomes produced in part by those choices.

I firmly believe we get something worthwhile out of every job we do, even if it is just the certain knowledge that we never want to do it again. You just have to look for that nugget of gold and polish it up. It could shine a ray in a new direction that makes all the professional difference in the world.

29. *I don't know what I want to do professionally. How do I figure that out?*

Educate yourself on the possibilities. Make a list of fields that you think might interest you and start researching them.

Visit a career counselor at the military education center or call one at Military OneSource and start your research today. Read about different careers and analyze your skills. You can do both in Chapter Two. Talk online or in person with others who work in the fields you're thinking about and get their perspectives.

30. *How can I balance being a single parent and working a full-time job while my spouse is deployed?*

It's not easy, but it's not impossible either. It can be difficult adjusting to your spouse's absence. Accept that there will be good days and not so good days ahead of you.

Before he or she leaves, it may help to figure out how you will keep in touch with one another while separated. Take care of the legal paperwork before s/he leaves. Make sure you have a power of attorney and your wills are updated.

Understand how you will manage family finances between the miles. Taking care of these kinds of details beforehand will save you from arguing on the phone when you are trying to figure out how the check bounced.

Arrange for additional back-up childcare if necessary for those times you have to work late or take a business trip. Revisit your existing support network and maybe add another name or two to the list.

Let your employer know that your spouse is going to be away for some time. At times when you need to leave work early to tend to domestic matters, it will be helpful to have the support of your employer.

Take care of yourself. Try to eat right, exercise, and get enough sleep. Don't isolate yourself in his or her absence. Stay involved with your children, your friends, and your job. Consider starting a diary in which you can journal your feelings and experiences.

Breathe in. Breathe out. Take it one day at a time.

Overseas Employment

31. We are being transferred overseas. Will I be able to get a job quickly?

Good question. It depends on **where** you're moving overseas. It can take a long time. If you depend on your paycheck stateside, save as much as you can before you move overseas.

For the most part, job opportunities on military installations overseas will be limited. If you are moving to a large military community, your chances will, of course, be better than if you are moving to smaller one or one that doesn't have any significant U.S. support structure in place.

Spouses who work overseas within military communities may work for the federal government in an appropriated (GS) or non-appropriated (NAF) position. They might also work for nonprofit organizations such as the Red Cross or the USO. There may be opportunities to work in contract positions, being paid in either U.S. dollars or host nation currency, in banking, education, or defense.

Job opportunities off of the military installation may be non-existent for you, depending on the Status of Forces Agreement (SOFA) that is negotiated between the host nation and the United States.

If you are able to work within the host nation, you will most likely be responsible for paying host nation taxes as well. You may need a host nation work permit, and you may need to be able to speak the local language as well.

32. We are stationed overseas and live in base housing. Can I sell products like baskets, lingerie, or cookware from our quarters?

You need to check with the installation's command to get the answer that applies to your community. If you can do it, you can be sure you won't be allowed to have products shipped to your APO or FPO mailbox because you are not permitted to use the postal service for your own business use. Hostesses for such parties usually get around that fine point by having their orders sent directly to the customers instead.

33. What is the SOFA and how does it affect me as far as employment is concerned?

The Status of Forces Agreements (SOFA) are agreements between the United States and other countries that establish the framework under which U.S. military servicemembers and their families can operate while residing in a foreign country. In some countries, spouses are not permitted to work off the military installation because of a SOFA. In others, it permits certain spouses to work within the host nation sans work permit. It doesn't, however, eliminate the reality of host nation taxes and federal reporting of foreign earned income. Bottom line – talk to the legal office on the military installation in the host nation where you're stationed. The employment readiness manager at the family support center might also be able to answer this for you.

34. How long will it take me to find a job overseas on the military installation?

Again, it depends on where you're going overseas. You have to remember that being stationed abroad is different from being stationed anywhere in the United States. Opportunities may be significantly limited.

Usually, you can count on at least a three-month to one-year job search time period. You may even meet other spouses who have given up the idea of working for a paycheck while stationed overseas.

If you should find yourself unable to land a paying job overseas, the key is to continue working in some way. There are usually ample opportunities to volunteer. Go back to school. Start working online. Make the time count even if you can't get the job you want.

Life Changes

35. My spouse was wounded in Afghanistan and I need to become the main family breadwinner now, but I'm not sure how to do that.

Life is not always fair, and this seems like one of those times for you and your family. Making such a big transition will no doubt take time, patience, and perseverance. I can imagine that you must be feeling overwhelmed by all the changes in your life.

There are many different resources that you can turn to for assistance. Military OneSource is one that comes to mind. The Transition Assistance Program/Disabled Transition Assistance Program is another.

The military family service and support center on the installation nearest you can also help you in many ways. If you don't live near an installation, visit Joint Services Support online for assistance (http://www.joint-servicessupport.org/).

36. I've been out of the job market for quite some time, raising my children but I'm ready to go back. How can I compete for jobs against others?

   1. Don't make the mistake of thinking you haven't been doing anything marketable. For example, if you have been volunteering in

the community, capitalize on those experiences and put them on your resume.

2. Get a good feel for your strengths and weaknesses. A career counselor or the exercises in Chapter Two can help you. Pay a visit to the employment readiness program manager on the installation for face-to-face assistance and access the many great tips on the subject provided on Military OneSource.

3. Sharpen any skills and knowledge for the types of jobs you are interested in doing. You can do this through a combination of volunteering and formal or informal job training. Read everything you can get your hands on related to the job(s) you are interested in pursuing.

4. Rebuild your network of contacts and your professional wardrobe.

5. Get your family members on board with your new direction. They are used to seeing you there for them when they leave for work or school in the morning and when they return in the afternoon. That may not be the case in the near future and you need to help them adjust.

6. Don't be hard on yourself. Going back to the workplace after a long period of unemployment can be tough mentally, physically, and emotionally. Don't try to master it the first week on the job. Give yourself time to adjust.

Transitioning or Retiring Out of the Military

37. My spouse is getting ready to get out of the military and is scheduled to attend a job search workshop on the base. Can I go, too?

Yes! Please go with your soon-to-be-civilian spouse. The process of getting out of the military, whether through retirement or not, is a big move. Two heads are so much better than one. You can both benefit from the knowledge and you can help each other every step of the way. You can use the transition assistance program (TAP/DTAP) services even after you've left the military lifestyle behind. To learn more about it, visit www.turbotap.org.

Education and Training

38. I started my degree program in one place and we are moving to another. Will my program transfer?

That depends on the school where you are earning your degree program. Be sure you coordinate with your academic advisor well in advance of any moves, preferably before you even enroll in a program.

Visit the education center on the military installation nearest you to identify the colleges and universities that participate in the Servicemembers Opportunities Colleges (SOC) consortium, enabling you to more easily move around and still finish your degree. You can learn more on SOC's website: http://www.soc.aascu.org/Default.html.

39. With unemployment so high and prospects so bleak, is it worth it to get a college degree?

Yes, it is. Go back to Chapter Two. Do not pass Go until you've read the part about how much people with and without a college education make over the course of lifetime. Then you may take action by heading to the military education center where you can get started on this goal.

40. Can I use my spouse's GI Bill to pay for my college degree?

Maybe, but it may depend on a few things such as how long your uniformed spouse has been on active duty and his or her future service commitments. To keep abreast of the latest on the subject, go to the Veterans Administration website: www.va.gov.

41. What scholarships are available to me as a military spouse?

There are a number of scholarships established for military spouses. Refer to Chapter Two, page 17, for a list of specific scholarships that you can search online.

42. What is a mentor and how can I get one?

A mentor is someone who shares the wisdom of his or her experience with you. It is someone who may be able to connect you to others, opening doors that you wouldn't be able to open on your own. A good mentor adds to your education and training.

Everyone should have a mentor or two whom she or he can call on occasionally for guidance. You may be able to find a mentor in your own community or you may have to look outside of it.

A mentor might be a former employer, teacher, or other business professional whom you know through your networking venues. It should be someone you respect and admire.

To land yourself a mentor, you have to ask the person to take on the role, clearly defining what you would like to get from them. Don't be offended if you are turned down; just ask if they can recommend someone else to you.

The ultimate goal, of course, is to become a mentor yourself. Give back the good that you receive to someone else.

10

Successfully Achieving Your Employment Goals: A Final Word

CONGRATULATIONS! You've made it to the last chapter of an essential career guide that can help you create the professional identity you seek. With the knowledge I hope you've gained in this book, you are now better prepared to handle the job market realities facing you today.

Throughout these pages, we have reviewed those external and internal challenges we spouses often confront as we try our best to make smart job choices in our mobile lives.

These, as you may painfully recall, are some of the obstacles we cope with:

- The perfect job opportunities don't always exist when we're ready for them in our lives. Someone else gets hired over us, someone already has the job, or the job doesn't exist.

- Circumstances beyond our control often cloud our vision and prevent us from reaching our professional goals on both the short and long-term fronts. Among other things, those circumstances may involve multiple deployments, reunions, relocations, growing families or aging ones. They could involve physical, mental, and emotional challenges as well.

- Personal financial obligations may stand in our way, preventing us from taking reasonable and calculated risks.

- Varying state licensure and certification requirements may impede our efforts to be consistently and gainfully employed with each PCS move.

The obstacles we deal with now and those that will surface later are real, and they are not going to get any smaller.

For the past decade, we have been a nation at war. As I write this chapter, President Obama has called an end to the Iraqi war and has said that all the troops stationed there will be home for the holidays. It will be, according to the president, "a season of homecomings."

It is, of course, the best news any military family could hear. Politics aside, we want our loved ones safe, sound, and close to us. On that point, it doesn't get any better.

Financially, however, things could get much worse for military service-members and their families in the next few years.

If we were to gaze into a crystal ball, we might see that as funds are ultimately shifted away from the DoD and into other areas, there will be stark differences in the level of program support to military spouses and families. Sources of funding and support you have grown accustomed to may or may not be available in the future. (Translation: Don't wait around to take advantage of any current programs. If you do, you may be completely out of luck.)

The truth is simple and ironically familiar: we just don't know what the future will hold.

To successfully deal with those employment obstacles and the uncertainty forever inherent in military life, to make those smart moves, we must rely on three attributes we military spouses possess.

1. The Voice Inside Ourselves

Smart job choices, strategies, and solutions are well within our reach despite the often overwhelming obstacles and our ever-changing military lifestyle realities.

You need only mindfully listen to that little voice inside yourself. It's the one that speaks to you when everything else is mercifully still, which may not happen often, so you have to be open to "hearing" that voice.

It is the voice that speaks the basic truth, telling us which choice to make or which strategy or solution will work the best for us regardless of how it has worked for someone else. It is also the voice we may choose to ignore because it doesn't always offer us the convenient solutions but the right ones.

Call it your gut instinct, intuition, or a sixth sense. Call it whatever term works for you but listen to it. It knows what it's talking about better than anyone else, and you should trust it completely.

2. Our Inner Scorecard

In addition to the inner voice we ignore too often, there is the proverbial scorecard we put far too much emphasis on in the first place.

Let's be honest. Everyone does it to a certain extent. We compare our professional progress to that of others. We don't always like what we see. We might feel that we are more educated and experienced than someone else who appears to have easily reached the professional level we ourselves have been struggling to attain. It can be disappointing, to say the least.

That is the negative essence of the "scorecard." Luckily for us, there is also a positive aspect to it.

As we look around and see what other spouses are doing in their jobs and in their careers, we get new ideas to consider and potentially act upon. This motivates us to look deep within ourselves and examine what we're doing professionally. In this way, the "scorecard" can encourage us to do better, reach higher, or change paths altogether.

Anything that spurs positive professional growth should be embraced with wild abandon. In the words of Martha Stewart, "It's a good thing."

3. Resiliency

Smart job choices, strategies, and solutions happen when you listen to your inner voice. They seem to magically occur when you stop negatively comparing yourself to someone else. They surface when you tap into the power of your very own secret weapon of resiliency.

In the past few years, there has been a large body of military-centric literature written for our benefit, reminding us about our impressive levels of resiliency. Designed to sustain and encourage us, books, articles, websites, and never-ending PowerPoint presentations in crowded conference rooms around the world remind us repeatedly that we military spouses are a resilient lot.

In other words, we have the ability to overcome stressful setbacks and formidable obstacles. More than most, we know how to maintain positive thoughts during times of adversity.

Resiliency has been so much part of our role as military spouses for so long now that it seems more like a second skin than a noun or adjective. What we sometimes fail to do, however, is wear that same resiliency in our pursuit of a better job or a career.

Being career-resilient means being able to adapt and change with the tides. It means being employable. You can move forward professionally on one coast or the other or even way over on the other side of the world. It might not mean moving forward, but sideways. In any event, it certainly means being open to the options. It means committing to the concept of continuous learning so that you are always improving and developing skills that can be used to further your career goals.

Resiliency means being flexible, carrying the concept of Gumby to new and improved heights. Flexibility is something you know how to do well in your military life; it is a quality that will also serve you well in your professional life.

* * *

So, there you have it: your inner voice, your "scorecard" perspective, and your level of career resiliency. Combined with the strategies and solutions contained in this book, these attributes can help you make smart job choices and achieve your professional goals in uncertain times!

Go-To Resources

YOU DON'T HAVE to have all the answers. You just need to know where to go to get them.

Bookmark and Visit Regularly

Military Homefront
www.militaryhomefront.dod.mil

Highlights and headlines you need to know about from the DoD. Subscribe to the free Military Community & Family Policy (MC&FP) eMagazine to stay informed about critical issues that may affect you as a member of the military family.

Military OneSource
www.militaryonesource.mil

Military OneSource is there for you 24/7/365 for just about any question or concern that comes to your mind. Think of them as a virtual family support center. Subscribe to free monthly newsletters on any number of topics, including Spouse Education and Careers.

Military Spouse Employment Partnership
www.msepjobs.militaryonesource.mil

This must-view/use resource not only helps you with how-to job search basics, but also enables you to apply for real jobs wherever you are stationed.

USA 4 Military Families
www.usa4militaryfamilies.dod.mil

You'll find information regarding the 10 key quality-of-life issues here along with information about partnership and initiatives between the DoD and the States.

Military Community and Family Policy can also be accessed through

Twitter: https://twitter.com/#!/MC_FP
Facebook: www.facebook.com/MCandFP

YouTube:	www.youtube.com/MCandFP
Flickr:	www.flickr.com/photos/mcfp

The National Resource Directory
https://www.nationalresourcedirectory.gov/

The mother ship all of national resources for servicemembers, veterans, wounded warriors, and family members.

Career Coaches/Services for Hire

CareerPro Global, Inc.
www.careerproplus.com

Janet Farley, Consultant & Author
Personalized Job Search and Career Planning
www.janetfarley.com

Jump into Life!
www.jumpintolife.net

The Military Spouse Coach: Krista Wells
Support Strategies and Solutions for Career and Life
http://militaryspousecoach.com

Military Spouse: Portable Career Planning
www.portablecareerplanning.com

The Resume Place (Federal Resume Assistance)
www.resume-place.com

Woman 2 Woman Career and Life Transition Coaching
http://woman2womanlifecoaching.com

Career Exploration

O*Net Online
www.onetonline.org

Occupational Outlook Handbook
www.bls.gov/oco/

Certifications and Licensing Information

All Nurses
www.allnurses.com

American Dental Hygienists' Association
www.adha.org

DoD – State Liaison Update (April 2010)
www.ncsl.org/documents/environ/EKringer0410.pdf

The Federation of State Boards of Physical Therapy
www.fsbpt.org

National Conference of State Legislatures
www.ncsl.org

Nursing World
www.nursingworld.org

Teachers Support Network
www.teacherssupportnetwork.com

Education and Scholarships, Grants, and Loans

Air Force Aid Society
www.afas.org

Army Emergency Relief
www.aerhq.org

Career Advancement Accounts
https://aiportal.acc.af.mil/mycaa/

Coast Guard Mutual Assistance
www.cgmahq.org

College Answer
www.collegeanswer.com

CollegeBoard
www.collegeboard.org

CollegeNET
www.collegenet.com

College Scholarships.org
www.collegescholarships.org

Department of Education
www.ed.gov

ECampus Tours
www.ecampustours.com

FastWeb: Paying for School Just Got Easier
www.fastweb.com

Federal Student Aid: Get Help Paying for College
www.fafsa.ed.gov

Navy-Marine Corps Relief Society
www.nmcrs.org

Peterson's – Your Comprehensive Guide to College Information
www.petersons.com

SallieMae
www.salliemae.com

Scholarship Programs of the Fisher House Foundation
www.militaryscholar.org

The SmartStudent Guide to Financial Aid
www.finaid.org

StaffordLoan.com
www.staffordloan.com

Voluntary Education Portal
http://apps.mhf.dod.mil/pls/psgprod/f?p=VOLED:HOME:0

Employment Sources on the Installation

Commissary
www.commissaries.com

Department of Defense Education Activity
www.Dodea.edu

The Exchange
www.shopmyexchange.com

Navy Exchange
www.mynavyexchange.com

USAJOBS
www.usajobs.com

Family and Employment Readiness Assistance

Air Force Community
www.afcommunity.af.mil

Amed Forces Crossroads
www.afcrossroads.com

Army Career and Alumni Program
https://www.hrc.army.mil/site/active/tagd/acap

Army OneSource
www.myarmyonesource.com

Career OneStop
www.careeronestop.org

Commander Navy Installations Cammand
www.cnic.navy.mil

Department of Labor
www.dol.gov

Marine Corps Community Services
www.usmc-mccs.org

Military OneSource.com
www.militaryonesource.com

Military Spouse Career Center
www.military.com/spouse

National Guard Bureau Joint Services Support
www.jointservicessupport.org

TurboTap
www.turbotap.org

Federal Jobs: Where to Find Them

USA Jobs
www.usajobs.gov

Air Force Civilian Service
www.afciviliancareers.com/home/

U.S. Army Civilian Personnel Online
http://cpol.army.mil

U.S. Coast Guard Civilian Careers
http://uscg.mil/civilian

Dept. of the Navy Civilian Human Resources
www.public.donhr.navy.mil

Networking: Professional and Social

Army Wife Network
www.armywifenetwork.com

Association of the U.S. Army Family Programs
www.ausa.org/family

CinCHouse.com
www.cinchouse.com

Military Officers Association of America
www.moaa.org

Military Spouse Business Association
www.milspousebiz.org

Military Spouse Corporate Career Network
www.msccn.org

Military Spouse Magazine
www.milspouse.com

National Military Family Association
www.militaryfamily.org

National Military Spouse Network
http://nationalmilitaryspousenetwork.org

Spouse Buzz
http://spousebuzz.com

PCS Move Survival Assistance

Military Youth on the Move
http://apps.mhf.dod.mil/pls/psgprod/f?p=MYOM:HOME:0

Military Installations
www.militaryinstallations.dod.mil

Plan My Move
https://apps.mhf.dod.mil/pls/psgprod/f?p=PMM:ENTRY:0

Self-Employment Assistance

IRS: Small Business and Self-Employed Tax Center
www.irs.gov/businesses/small/index.html

SCORE: For the Life of Your Business
www.score.org

Small Business Administration
www.sba.gov

Social Security: If You Are Self-Employed
www.ssa.gov/pubs/10022.html

U.S. Department of Labor: Self-Employment Assistance
http://workforcesecurity.doleta.gov/unemploy/self.asp

USA.Gov for the Self-Employed
www.usa.gov/Business/Self_Employed.shtml

Unemployment Insurance

Unemployment Compensation for Military Spouses by State
(18 May 2011)
www.ncsl.org/?TabId=13331

US Department of Labor Unemployment Information
http://workforcesecurity.doleta.gov/unemploy/

Index

Career Resources

THE FOLLOWING resources are available directly from Impact Publications. Full descriptions of each title – as well as downloadable catalogs, DVDs, software, games, posters, and related products – can be found at www.impactpublications.com. Complete this form or list the titles, include shipping (see the formula at the end), enclose payment, and send your order to:

IMPACT PUBLICATIONS
9104 Manassas Drive, Suite N
Manassas Park, VA 20111-5211 USA
1-800-361-1055 (orders only)
Tel. 703-361-7300 or Fax 703-335-9486
Email address: query@impactpublications.com
Quick & easy online ordering: www.impactpublications.com

Orders from individuals must be prepaid by check, money order, or major credit card. We accept telephone, fax, and email orders.

Qty.	Titles	Price	TOTAL
Featured Title			
_____	The Military Spouse's Employment Guide	$17.95	_____
Military Spouses and Families			
_____	1001 Things to Love About Military Life	19.99	_____
_____	After the War Zone: A Practical Guide for Returning Troops	14.95	_____
_____	Army Wives	13.95	_____
_____	Chicken Soup for the Military Wife's Soul	14.95	_____
_____	Complete Idiot's Guide to Life as a Military Spouse	12.95	_____
_____	Family's Guide to the Military for Dummies	19.99	_____
_____	Help! I'm a Military Spouse – I Get a Life Too!	15.95	_____
_____	Heroes at Home	13.99	_____
_____	Home Fires Burning	14.95	_____
_____	Homefront Club	21.95	_____
_____	In Harm's Way	14.95	_____
_____	Married to the Military	14.00	_____
_____	Military Spouse Finance Guide	19.95	_____
_____	Military Spouse's Complete Guide to Career Success	17.95	_____
_____	The Mocha Manual to Military Life	14.99	_____
_____	Navy Spouse's Guide	21.95	_____
_____	Once a Warrior, Always a Warrior	18.95	_____
_____	Operation Military Family	19.95	_____
_____	Separated By Duty, United In Love	9.95	_____
_____	Surviving Deployment	19.95	_____
_____	Today's Military Wife	19.95	_____

Qty.	Titles	Price	TOTAL
Military and Spousal Pocket Guides			
_____	Best Jobs amd Employers for Military Spouses Pocket Guide	2.95	_____
_____	Best Jobs for Military-to-Civilian Transition Pocket Guide	2.95	_____
_____	Military Family Benefits Pocket Guide	2.95	_____
_____	Military Family Education Pocket Guide	2.95	_____
_____	Military Family Legal Pocket Guide	2.95	_____
_____	Military Financial Independence and Retirement Pocket Guide	2.95	_____
_____	Military Personal Finance Pocket Guide	2.95	_____
_____	Military Recreation and Travel Pocket Guide	2.95	_____
_____	Military Spouse's Employment Pocket Guide	2.95	_____
_____	Military Spouse's Map Through the Maze Pocket Guide	2.95	_____
_____	Military-to-Civilian Transition Pocket Guide	2.95	_____
_____	Military-to-Federal Employment Pocket Guide	2.95	_____
_____	The Quick Job Finding Pocket Guide	2.95	_____
_____	Top Military-Friendly Employers Pocket Guide	2.95	_____
_____	Veteran's Business Start-Up Pocket Guide	2.95	_____
Military Benefits			
_____	Claims Denied: How to Appeal a VA Denial of Benefits	16.95	_____
_____	Complete Idiot's Guide to Your Military and Veterans Benefits	18.95	_____
_____	Financial Aid for Veterans, Military Personnel, and		
	Their Dependents	40.00	_____
_____	The Military Advantage	26.95	_____
_____	Servicemember's Guide to a College Degree	14.95	_____
_____	Veteran's Benefits for Dummies	19.99	_____
_____	Veteran's Guide to Benefits	16.95	_____
_____	Veteran's Survival Guide	17.95	_____
Military in Transition			
_____	Expert Resumes for Military-to-Civilian Transition	16.95	_____
_____	Job Search: Marketing Your Military Experience	19.95	_____
_____	Marketing Yourself for a Second Career DVD	49.95	_____
_____	Military Guide to Financial Independence and Retirement	17.95	_____
_____	Military-to-Civilian Resumes and Letters	21.95	_____
_____	Military-to-Civilian Career Transition Guide	14.95	_____
_____	Military-to-Civilian Transition Guide	13.95	_____
_____	Military-to-Civilian Transition Inventory (package of 25)	49.95	_____
_____	Military to Federal Career Guide	18.95	_____
_____	Military Spouse's Complete Guide to Career Success	17.95	_____
_____	Military Transition to Civilian Success	21.95	_____
_____	Out of Uniform	24.95	_____
_____	Quick Military Transition Guide (package of 10)	46.95	_____
Government and Security Jobs			
_____	Book of U.S. Government Jobs	27.95	_____
_____	Complete Guide to Public Employment	19.95	_____

Qty.	Titles	Price	TOTAL
_____	Federal Law Enforcement Careers	19.95	_____
_____	Federal Resume Guide Book	21.95	_____
_____	Post Office Jobs	24.95	_____
_____	Ten Steps to a Federal Job	28.95	_____

Testing and Assessment

_____	Career, Aptitude, and Selections Tests	17.95	_____
_____	Career Match	15.00	_____
_____	Discover What You're Best At	14.95	_____
_____	Do What You Are	18.99	_____
_____	Employment Personality Tests Decoded	16.99	_____
_____	The Everything Career Tests Book	12.95	_____
_____	I Want to Do Something Else, But I'm Not Sure What It Is	15.95	_____
_____	Military-to-Civilian Transition Inventory (package of 25)	49.95	_____
_____	Now, Discover Your Strengths	30.00	_____
_____	What Should I Do With My Life?	16.00	_____
_____	What Type Am I?	16.00	_____
_____	What's Your Type of Career?	21.95	_____

Interviews

_____	101 Dynamite Questions to Ask At Your Job Interview	13.95	_____
_____	101 Great Answers to the Toughest Interview Questions	12.99	_____
_____	301 Best Questions to Ask On Your Interview	14.95	_____
_____	301 Smart Answers to Tough Interview Questions	12.95	_____
_____	Best Answers to 201 Most Frequently Asked Interview Questions	14.95	_____
_____	Can I Wear My Nose Ring to the Interview?	13.95	_____
_____	Everything Practice Interview Book	14.95	_____
_____	I Can't Believe They Asked Me That!	17.95	_____
_____	Instant Interviews	16.95	_____
_____	Interview Magic	18.95	_____
_____	Job Interview Tips for People With Not-So-Hot Backgrounds	14.95	_____
_____	Job Interview Phrase Book	10.95	_____
_____	Job Interviews for Dummies	16.99	_____
_____	KeyWords to Nail the Job Interview	17.95	_____
_____	Nail the Job Interview!	14.95	_____
_____	The Savvy Interviewer	10.95	_____
_____	Tell Me About Yourself	14.95	_____
_____	Win the Interview, Win the Job	15.95	_____
_____	Winning Job Interviews	12.99	_____
_____	You Have 3 Minutes!	21.95	_____
_____	You Should Hire Me!	15.95	_____

Social Media

_____	Find a Job Through Social Networking	14.95	_____
_____	How to Find a Job on LindedIn, Facebook, Twitter, MySpace, and Other Social Networks	18.95	_____

Qty.	Titles	Price	TOTAL
_____	Twitter Job Search Guide	14.95	_____
_____	Web 2.0 Job Finder	15.99	_____

Salary Negotiations

_____	101 Salary Secrets	12.95	_____
_____	250 Best-Paying Jobs	16.95	_____
_____	Get a Raise in 7 Days	14.95	_____
_____	Give Me More Money!	17.95	_____
_____	Salary Negotiation Tips for Professionals	16.95	_____
_____	Salary Tutor	13.99	_____
_____	Secrets of Power Salary Negotiating	13.99	_____

Attitude and Motivation

_____	100 Ways to Motivate Yourself	14.99	_____
_____	Attitude Is Everything	16.99	_____
_____	Change Your Thinking, Change Your Life	19.95	_____
_____	Goals!	18.95	_____
_____	Little Gold Book of YES! Attitude	19.99	_____
_____	Success Principles	16.95	_____

Resumes and Letters

_____	101 Great Tips for a Dynamite Resume	13.95	_____
_____	201 Dynamite Job Search Letters	19.95	_____
_____	Best KeyWords for Resumes, Cover Letters, & Interviews	17.95	_____
_____	Best Resumes and CVs for International Jobs	24.95	_____
_____	Best Resumes for $100,000+ Jobs	24.95	_____
_____	Best Resumes for People Without a Four-Year Degree	19.95	_____
_____	Blue-Collar Resume and Job Hunting Guide	15.95	_____
_____	Competency-Based Resumes	13.99	_____
_____	Cover Letter Magic	18.95	_____
_____	Cover Letters for Dummies	16.99	_____
_____	Cover Letters That Knock 'Em Dead	12.95	_____
_____	Create Your Digital Portfolio	19.95	_____
_____	Expert Resumes for Baby Boomers	16.95	_____
_____	Expert Resumes for Career Changers	16.95	_____
_____	Expert Resumes for Computer and Web Jobs	16.95	_____
_____	Expert Resumes for People Returning to Work	16.95	_____
_____	Haldane's Best Cover Letters for Professionals	15.95	_____
_____	Haldane's Best Resumes for Professionals	15.95	_____
_____	High Impact Resumes and Letters	19.95	_____
_____	Military-to-Civilian Resumes and Letters	21.95	_____
_____	Nail the Cover Letter!	17.95	_____
_____	Nail the Resume!	17.95	_____
_____	Resume, Application, and Letter Tips for People With Hot and Not-So-Hot Backgrounds	17.95	_____
_____	Resumes for Dummies	16.99	_____

Qty.	Titles	Price	TOTAL
_____	Resumes That Knock 'Em Dead	12.95	_____
_____	The Savvy Resume Writer	12.95	_____
_____	Step-By-Step Resumes	19.95	_____
_____	Winning Letters That Overcome Barriers to Employment	17.95	_____

Networking

_____	Fine Art of Small Talk	16.95	_____
_____	Little Black Book of Connections	19.95	_____
_____	Masters of Networking	18.95	_____
_____	Networking for People Who Hate Networking	16.95	_____
_____	Never Eat Alone	24.95	_____
_____	One Phone Call Away	24.95	_____
_____	Power Networking	14.95	_____
_____	The Savvy Networker	13.95	_____
_____	Work the Pond!	15.95	_____

SUBTOTAL
Virginia residents add 5% sales tax   _____

POSTAGE/HANDLING $5.00 +
($5 for first product and 9% of SUBTOTAL)   additional:

9% of SUBTOTAL
(Include an additional 15% if shipping   _____
outside the continental United States)   _____

TOTAL ENCLOSED   _____

SHIP TO:

Name: _____

Address: _____

_____

_____

PAYMENT METHOD:

☐ I enclose check/money order for $ _____ made payable to
IMPACT PUBLICATIONS.

☐ Please charge $ _____ to my credit card:

☐ Visa ☐ MasterCard ☐ American Express ☐ Discover

Card #_____Expiration date: ____/____

Signature_____

Military-Friendly Pocket Guides

Inexpensive, Practical, and Engaging Action Guides for Success!

User-friendly resources from 59¢ to $2.95 each!

- Written by leading career/life skills experts
- Engaging 64-page, reader-friendly action guides
- Fit conveniently into pockets or handbags (3 7/8" x 4 7/8")
- Focus on making smart decisions and using key resources
- Jam-packed with compelling checklists, tests, and examples
- Can be customized around client needs (Special Edition option)

Quantity discounts on all pocket guides

Per unit discounts/costs		Quantity costs	
10-24 copies	20% ($2.36)	10 copies	$23.60
25-49 copies	30% ($2.06)	25 copies	$51.63
50-99 copies	40% ($1.77)	50 copies	$88.50
100-499 copies	50% ($1.48)	100 copies	$147.50
500-999 copies	55% ($1.33)	500 copies	$663.75
1,000-4,999 copies	60% ($1.18)	1,000 copies	$1,180.00
100,000+ copies	80% ($0.59)	100,000 copies	$59,000.00

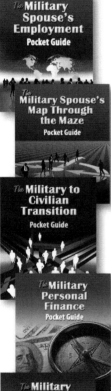

The Military Spouse's Employment Pocket Guide
Ron Krannich, Ph.D.
This pocket guide assists spouses in quickly finding and keeping a job. It helps them:

- organize key job search information
- conduct interviews, follow up, and negotiate
- specify transferable skills, references, and networks
- write winning resumes, letters, and applications
- survive, thrive, and advance on the job

It also covers important information relating to education and training, attitudes and goals, barriers to employment, jobs and employers, federal jobs, Internet resources, employment assistance, contacts, and resources. 64 pages. 2009. ISBN 978-1-57023-303-6. **$2.95**

The Military Spouse's Map Through the Maze Pocket Guide
Trudy S. Woodring and Ronald L. Krannich, Ph.D.
From relocating, volunteering, and handling family finances to raising children, using base services, and managing deployment, spouses often face a daunting task of knowing what to do and where to go for assistance. This handy pocket guide includes a wealth of useful information and tips on navigating the military maze. It covers such important subjects as base services, TRICARE, pay, benefits, education, health care, deployment, personal finances, jobs and careers, etiquette, PTSD, injuries, travel, relocation, moving overseas, retirement, and much more. 64 pages. 2009. ISBN 978-1-57023-304-3. **$2.95**

The Military-to-Civilian Transition Pocket Guide
Ron Krannich, Ph.D.
Our bestseller with more than 500,000 copies in print! Filled with the latest strategies and timeless tips for launching a successful military-to-civilian transition, this revealing guide helps users:

- identify transferable military-to-civilian skills
- locate the best military-friendly companies
- assess skills and state goals
- complete applications and write resumes and letters
- attend and work job fairs effectively
- network, interview, and negotiate compensation

It also covers such important subjects as starting a business, surviving on the job, planning for retirement, documenting experience, finding a federal job, and identifying references. Jam-packed with engaging checklists, tips, examples, and exercises. 64 pages. 2009. ISBN 978-1-57023-305-0. **$2.95**

The Military Personal Finance Pocket Guide:
Smart Decisions for Securing Your Financial Future
Trudy S. Woodring and Ronald L. Krannich, Ph.D.
This practical guide is designed to improve the financial I.Q. of military personnel and their families by offering numerous insider tips on financial planning, budgeting, investment, insurance, banking, borrowing, tax strategies, VA benefits, retirement, and much more. Shows how to quickly get ahead of the financial game with sound advice on setting goals and making smart financial decisions that will last for a lifetime! Jam-packed with engaging checklists, tips, examples, exercises, and recommended resources. 64 pages. 2010. ISBN 978-1-57023-308-1. **$2.95**

The Military Family Benefits Pocket Guide
Ronald L. Krannich, Ph.D. and Trudy S. Woodring
As a member of the military, you and your family are entitled to many benefits that you've earned. However, many individuals are unclear about their immediate- and long-term benefits and how to best access them. This handy guide succinctly summarizes the major benefits available to servicemembers, veterans, and their families. It covers military pay, health care (TRICARE and VA), housing, exchanges, child care, education, legal assistance, travel, family support, spousal employment assistance, discounts, retirement, and much, much more. Includes key websites and contact information. Fits conveniently into pockets and handbags for quick reference and review. 64 pages. 2011. ISBN 978-157023-317-3. **$2.95**

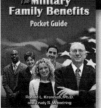

ORDERS: 1.800.361.1055 or www.impactpublications.com